The
John Hannam Interviews
More Wight Connections

The
John Hannam Interviews
More Wight Connections

More revealing stories behind John's
memorable interviews with past and
present Isle of Wight people

To TERRY

BEST WISHES

John Hannam

This book is dedicated to
Ronnie and Roddy Hannam

Ronnie and Roddy Hannam

Personal thanks to those who have always given me so much support.

Roy and Ena Hannam, my parents, my late wife, Heather, Sean and Caroline, Celia and John Vosper,
Diane and Peter Eames, Paul and Shauna Shutler and my partner, Roberta Crismass. I would also like to thank many close friends for their belief in me.

Grateful thanks to the *Isle of Wight County Press* for the use of so many of their photographs.

First published 2019 by John Hannam. Copyright © John Hannam

Book design by Mike Lambert, Freshwater, Isle of Wight PO40 9PP

Printed by Short Run Press Limited
25 Bittern Road, Sowton Industrial Estate, Exeter, Devon EX2 7LW

ISBN 978-0-9504126-7-2

ALSO AVAILABLE are John Hannam's books recalling his interviews with pop stars from the '50s, '60s and '70s and those with the stars of stage and screen past and present.
Plus John's first book revealing the stories behind the memorable interviews with past and present Isle of Wight people.

Contents

John Hannam

John with Celia Imrie

BACK IN 1974 when John began interviewing local and famous people, as a freelance journalist and broadcaster, he made a policy that he would only undertake in-person interviews. Over the years this may have lost him a few huge names but he has bravely stuck to his principals. For John, actually meeting his guests is of paramount importance. Even in his many years as a showbusiness feature writer he has always applied the same rule.

John thrives on doing hours of research for many interviews and has a friendly technique, which has been praised by many people over the past 45 years. Many have gone out of their way to congratulate him. John also prides himself on being a member of the old school of chat show hosts. He's had no desire to be the star of the show or to use his guests as pure fodder for cheap laughs. Private lives have never been on his agenda and his interviewees have always trusted him profusely. So much so, that on occasions, they have just opened up to reveal unexpected stories.

John has gained such a high reputation within the entertainment industry and Radio 2 have used around 20 of his archive recordings for their national radio shows. His archive is rated as one of the best in the British Isles. With over 5000 interviews to his name, including hundreds of Islanders, it's easy to see why.

A few years ago John brought out two CDs featuring stories from some of the Isle of Wight's best-loved characters. The success of these two eventually led him to *The Wight Connections*. Now comes this new book, *More Wight Connections*, with the extra bonus of some wonderful local archive pictures of past Island groups and entertainers.

This book features the stories behind another 100 of his acclaimed interviews with local people and he reveals memorable moments with Marius Goring, Henry Barney, Martin Woodward, Ian Dockray, Maurice Gilliam, Andrew Turner, Colin and Mavis Norris, Jeremy Irons, Gary Bachelor and many others.

Luckily, over 45 years, John has made many friends, some famous and others just delightful local Islanders. He just loves people and has built up a reputation of being fully trustworthy and a perfect professional.

John's new and old archive interviews can be heard all over the world on regular new online podcasts. Links can be obtained from John's website www.johnhannam.com plus the IW Radio website and leading podcast sites like Anchor FM and Spotify.

John with Laura Michelle Kelly

Foreword by Mark King

HAVING HAD the pleasure of knowing John for many years, I can now say there are few authors on the Isle of Wight who have a better knowledge of the Island's many diverse characters, be they in the public eye or local heroes, who contribute so much to the fabric of Island life.

Since we met way back in 1980, John has been a joy to chat to.

He's always positive and genuinely interested in whatever is happening in and around our towns and villages. This is clearly evident in this his latest book.

I wish you luck mate.

Mark King

Mark King with Level 42 at Ryde in 1980

Introduction – The Hannam Family

John Hannam

I AM PROUD to be an Islander and as this is going to be my last book, I want to pay tribute to my family. They have been a source of comfort to me for so many years. Their support has been so instrumental in what I may have achieved. Personally, I have surpassed my wildest dreams. From being a somewhat timid and shy teenager, who didn't like meeting people or even eating out in restaurants, I have gone on to enjoy a remarkable life. I am still conscious of the occasions, during my 20s, when I had to lie in a darkened room because of my complete lack of confidence. I was extremely low at times. My late wife, Heather, helped me to believe in myself. In later years I repaid her by introducing her to some of her favourite stars. I can still remember her quiet excitement as she met Russ Conway, Frankie Vaughan, Nigel Havers, Frankie Howerd, Acker Bilk, Bobby Vee and a few others.

Here are members of the Hannam family in my lifetime.

John Hannam

Ernest and Caroline Hannam – my grandparents.

Roy and Ena Hannam – my parents.

Celia – my sister – as the East Cowes Carnival Queen.

With my wife Heather.

Sean – my journalist son – with his wife Susie.

Caroline – my theatre head of wardrobe daughter – with Strictly Come Dancing's Vincent and Flavia.

Three generations of the Hannam family.

CHAPTER 1

Gary Bachelor

I FIRST GOT TO KNOW Gary Bachelor through a mutual friend – the late Wally Malston. Gary was at Cowes Denmark Road School with Wally, who went on to become one of the most prolific comedy scriptwriters in Britain. Anyone who wrote for Bob Monkhouse, Ted Rogers, Jimmy Tarbuck and Bruce Forsyth had reached the pinnacle of his profession. Gary was so proud of his old pal – as were so many of us.

When I first interviewed Gary, back in 1988, for my Sports Personality column in the *Weekly Post*, he had a unique record. In 12 cup finals the then Southern Vectis general manager had never been on the losing side. That list included six football finals, two golf finals and one each in cricket, bridge, crib and darts.

He told me, back in 1988: "I was never a natural. In every sport I've ever played it's been a struggle. I've had to overcome my lack of talent by keenness, determination and a will to win."

Gary failed his 11 plus and ended up at Cowes Secondary – and the same happened to me a few years later. In his business life, Gary had that same attitude he'd developed in sport. He began life as an office boy in J S Whites and ended up the boss of Southern Vectis. His years with our bus company really put them on the map.

Just before I'd interviewed Gary about his sporting life, I'd been flattered to be the only journalist to ride on a bus with Anita Dobson, who played Angie Watts in *EastEnders*. Thanks to Gary, I sat next to Anita when the company named a bus after her. We went on a tour around Newport and I gave her a kind of commentary but was not allowed to interview her. Not even Gary could persuade her manager to bend the rules set up by the *EastEnders* management, with regard to interviews. At least she brought Gary a Valentine card. Since Anita left the show I have interviewed her on two occasions and she is such a lovely lady.

Gary Bachelor with Anita Dobson

Gary made his own stage appearances as a member of the Wight Harmony Barbershop Chorus and they went on the win a national final.

In the Cowes area and beyond Gary was famous for his fantastic summer parties. He had a huge garden and a superb indoor swimming pool. Heather and I were added to the list of regulars. We did have a problem. Saturday nights were always busy for me with local shows to cover and stars to interview. It meant we had to come late – and not in fancy dress. I don't think it went down too well.

During my life I have always admired Islanders who have created their success by hard work and determination. Gary is the perfect example.

On many occasions he would ring me to tip me off about a story.

When I did a *John Hannam Meets* celebration for the life of Wally Malston, Gary was one of the first to volunteer to come on air and talk about his old pal.

I do have a favourite Gary Bachelor story. It concerns the game of bridge, Fratton Park and his pals Derek Flux, Johnny Williams and Colin Lane.

"We began playing bridge on the boat going over to watch Pompey play Preston. It continued in the stand before the match, at half-time, on the ferry back and then on the bus to Cowes. There was still no result so we went to one of our homes to finish it."

CHAPTER 2

Geoffrey Hughes & Jet Harris

Geoffrey Hughes

SADLY BOTH Geoffrey Hughes and Jet Harris have passed on. For many years they were fans of each other, without knowing it. Then came a chance meeting in a Southampton hospital. They were both living on the Island but had never met. The chance meeting came when they were both in wheelchairs recovering from treatment. They were both outside having a smoke. Geoff was signing an autograph for a nurse and then she saw Jet and asked him as well. There were only three wheelchairs in a row. When Jet realised who it was in another wheelchair he was heard to say "bloody hell there's Onslow." They became instant pals.

Knowing them both as friends, I got hold of this story and invited Jet to come back on my radio show – and asked him to bring his new friend. What a Sunday lunchtime that was.

It quickly became a mutual admiration society. Jet, who was the first electric bass icon in Britain, when he was in the original Shadows, had all the girls swooning over his moody good looks. The guys around the country also loved the Shads and wanted to play like them. There was a young kid from Liverpool who dreamed about playing in that fantastic group – but he turned to acting instead. You must have guessed by now. It was a council house boy named Geoffrey Hughes.

He told me: "Everybody of my age who lived in Liverpool was in a group and we all had guitars and equipment on hire purchase. I played in little church halls with a group called The Strangers. Jet Harris was such an influence on us, as were all the Shadows."

When Jet was a young guy he always wanted to be an actor – and that didn't mean wearing a Greek skirt in a Cliff Richard movie. He certainly had the looks for a movie star. He envied Geoffrey for all those great television roles in *Coronation Street*, *Keeping Up Appearances*, *Heartbeat* and *The Royle Family*.

"Geoffrey does what I always wanted to do, act. I'd love to have been an actor and I know lots of actors who wanted to become guitar players," said Jet.

Neither of them were theatre 'luvvies.'

"Both of us shouldn't really be in showbiz, to be quite honest. We're too ordinary." said Jet.

Geoff added: "We've both got away with it for a few years."

There was no doubt they both made the right decision to move to the Isle of Wight.

"When you move to the Island you never want to leave. I don't want to go to the 'north island'. The other day I turned down the chance to go back into *Coronation Street* because I didn't want to be away from home. I did all that for 40 years," admitted Geoff.

Jet Harris

Jet loved the Island and its people. Those sell-out concerts at the Medina proved that. He also loved playing petanque in a local league and, like Geoff, he loved the Island's wildlife.

Geoff also set up a very successful small local business on the Island which was another reason he never wanted to leave.

It was such a privilege to have known them both. They were always happy to oblige with a few favours, particularly for charity.

CHAPTER 3

Eddie Leal

HOW WOULD MANY senior citizens have celebrated their 70th birthday, back in 1992? The odd pint in their local, a tea dance, a Darby and Joan bun fight or an evening in with a favourite movie and a glass of wine. Well, in Eddie Leal's case he went for a run and kept on running for a few more years. He even celebrated his special birthday year by running to the top of Ben Nevis and down again.

On our last interview he told me he had actually run 84,000 miles during his life. Every week you could add another 40 miles to that total. In my days as a Ryde Harrier I used to go off faster than Eddie Leal, in the hope of finishing ahead of him. That never happened. In sight of the finishing line, he would just come by. It was a back I was used to seeing. Mind you, in my early days I could beat him over a mile. He was really a distance man.

Eddie was a marvel and such great fun to be with. He was born in Havenstreet and his earliest running was to and from school, in big black boots. That was back in the 1920s.

"In those days there was no tarmac roads, gas, electricity or sewers," reflected Eddie. It was such a rarity to even see a car. Now it's miracle if there's not a car in sight."

Eddie began running in the RAF and after the war he was one of seven cross country runners who helped form Ryde Harriers. They had a basement room in the Welby Institute. There was a single bulb light, one gas ring and a tin bath. Someone put the gas ring on around 11am and the bath water was ready by 3-30. The winner of the race got the luxury of a clean bath. The last man home sat in a mud pack. On three occasions Eddie was the Island cross country champion.

He was a local copper for a few years but then transferred to the Metropolitan Police and that was where he started to run marathons. Once he ran the 53 mile London to Brighton race in a pair of thin plimsolls, that cost him just under 20 pence.

After moving back home, his idea of a local marathon led people to think he'd gone out of his mind. Ed was rather clever. He suddenly got all the local dignitaries on his side. He'd invited the Duke of Wellington, then the governor of the Island, to start the race. The Portsmouth News sponsored the event. That was in 1957 – and it's still going strong.

In one really hot year an official was asked who was the Sikh seen running through Wootton? The competitor with his head and face completely hidden was actually born in Havenstreet. He was, in fact, E Leal.

Many will remember Eddie as the Island's countryside officer. He was so keen and our footpaths were never overgrown.

Eddie actually founded the Fell Runners Association. Now they have thousands of members. Once he finished a race at the top of Mount Snowdon. Tired and wet, like the other runners, he was looking forward to the train ride back down the mountain. The inclement weather halted the train and he had to find the quickest way down to collapse into his tent.

During the latter part of his life he became quite a serious ballroom dancer – and was rather good.

At the age of 70, did he have advice for veteran runners?

"As you get older you need to be more careful. The art is to run enough to keep healthy and in trim and not to do too much to wear yourself out."

He would be pleased to know that I have followed that wise advice.

CHAPTER 4

June Ring

I LOVE happy endings in movies, television dramas and real life. I have always felt that Yarmouth's June Ring has provided her very own, which has helped so many people. She bravely fought off cancer and eventually succeeded in obtaining her dream of seeing the Island have its own Wessex Cancer Support Centre. With her fundraising team she also helped to raise thousands of pounds towards the St Mary's Chemotherapy Unit. June spends her life helping others and has a heart of pure gold.

Our recent interviews have revealed her stories of being a much-loved barmaid in Island pubs. I have enjoyed finding out about the other life of June Ring.

After moving to the Island in 1967, she eventually took a job at the Royal Standard in Freshwater. That changed her life in more ways than one. One regular successfully chatted her up – and married her. It was a far cry from being a London civil servant and wearing twin sets and pearls.

June was keen to get her own pub and a drayman came up with the suggestion of the Hole In The Wall at Ventnor. Her and husband Dick had no money but that didn't put her off. She went to a bank manager, where she didn't even have an account, to ask for £2000. Being almost honest, she told him Dick had an account with them. Mind you, there was only £1 in it. For her cheek, they were given the money.

"It was something of a shock and many of the girls wore skirts with high silver boots and skull and crossbow jackets. Everyone seemed to have a tattoo. I also learnt a few new swear words in the first couple of days," said June.

They put a swear box on the bar and in six weeks had enough to treat the nearby St Catherine's School to a Christmas party – and buy a present for every pupil. It proved very touching – as every child at the school sent a thank you note.

"The customers were brilliant people with hearts of gold and, at times, I had to try and repair broken romances and also clean up new tattoos before they went home. Once I had to sew up a man's trousers as he'd split them before going on a hot date"

My favourite story was the day June sold Dick's dinner to a hungry customer. They didn't serve meals, just snacks. The smell of rabbit stew was just too much for one guy. So she sold him Dick's dinner and gave her old man pilchard sandwiches.

Eventually they went back to the Royal Standard but this time as mine hosts. They loved every minute and had to be very discreet at certain times – enough said.

Sadly, June was diagnosed with cancer whilst running the pub and she spent six weeks travelling to Netley Castle, near Southampton, and just came home for weekends. On her two days back home she got back into pub life and made meals for the following week and did all she could to help. They did appreciate some wonderful help from friends and customers.

After recovering from her illness, June was listening to Radio Solent and the news that Netley Hospital was to close. She was heard on-air pleading the case for Islanders and was asked by the Wessex Cancer Trust to raise money for the Island. The rest is history and hundreds of people have a lot to thank her for.

I love her company but have one regret. I've never seen her wearing a twin set and pearls. I'd prefer that to eating rabbit stew!

CHAPTER 5

Craig Douglas
The Terry Perkins Years

THE NAME OF Newport-born Craig Douglas was known all around the world, following his success as a pop star. To thousands of Islanders he was known as Terry Perkins – and still is by people of a certain age. After leaving Priory Boys School, being part of a large family of nine children, including three sets of twins, he needed a job to help support the family. He found that at Bill Strickland's farm in Calbourne.

Terry was actually born, with his twin brother Tony, in Prospect Road, Newport. The locals had another name for it. They dubbed it 'Incubator Alley.' In other words, there were a lot of children born in that small cul-de-sac near the old Newport Market. Later the Perkins family moved up the hill to the new Pan Estate.

Barton Boys, before they moved upmarket to Priory Boys, had a feared reputation as a schoolboy football team. I can vouch for that. One day around 100 yards from my home in Old Road, East Cowes, playing for Grange Road School, I bent my back six times taking the ball out of the net at Saro Sports ground. I will say this only once – Terry Perkins scored three of them. It's funny – he's never let me forget that. In that team were some superb young footballers like Keith Mitchell, Barry Foster, Monty Burton and Brian Greening (yes, even he was young once!). One of Barton's most popular teachers, Nobby Clark, lived 50 yards from me.

Terry got into music by accident – and it was all down to his lovely mum, Milly.

"I got in from the milk round one day and my mother said there was a letter for me. I'd never had one before. I opened it and read about a heat of a talent contest at the Medina Cinema, Newport. It said I was due to appear, which was quite a shock."

Young Terry had only previously sung on his milk round. He won the heat and in November 1957 won the grand final. It was to change his life for ever.

The Commodore Cinema, in Ryde, and the Medina were run by a guy called Robin Britten. He was rather astute and needed a couple of second opinions, as to whether Terry had a possible future in the pop music side of showbusiness. His second opinions turned out to be two top London agents, Bunny Lewis and his wife Janique Joelle. They came to watch him perform and sensed he had something different to offer, as a ballad singer. At that time, the British pop industry was swamped by potential rock 'n' roll stars, following the trend set by Tommy Steele. We had one on the Island called Johnny Vincent. His story is in the previous first edition of *The Wight Connections*, published in 2018.

Terry Perkins, along with Johnny Vincent and the Island's top skiffle group, The Nomads, were invited to appear in a week-long variety show at the Empire Theatre, Portsmouth. Terry was billed as 'The Boy With The Golden Voice.' It was a professional show and topping the bill was popular singer Maxine Daniels. Later her brother, Kenny Lynch, found fame as a singer.

Bunny and Janique did realise his potential and immediately sent him to a top class singing teacher and for elocution lessons. It was deemed his rustic Island accent needed to be refined. The name Terry Perkins was not box-office, either, so he became Craig Douglas. Then came dancing and acting lessons. They sensed he could become an all-round entertainer, beyond any pop success. They were right. He had a dozen hits and sold five million records and his career as an entertainer lasted until 2010, when he was confined to a wheelchair with vasculitis. This eventually brought a premature end to a marvellous career. Well done Perky!

CHAPTER 6

Colin and Mavis Norris

WHEN I FIRST MET Colin and Mavis Norris they were running their Norris Stores in Niton. I called on their shop when I worked for United Biscuits. None of us could ever have imagined that years later we would be talking to thousands of Islanders, via the airwaves, and not about Jaffa Cakes or Hob Nobs. When I went full time in the media they were delighted to rekindle old village memories.

In a way, Colin was lucky to even get to meet Mavis. Back in the old days he and his mates would get into mischief. During the last war, the Blackgang landslide area was used as an army firing range. They even found a Bren gun on a tripod left there by a careless soldier.

"We borrowed it and went down to the beach and fired tracer bullets out over the sea. When we found out the soldier was going to get his Christmas leave cancelled we took it back and told them we'd had found it in a hedge," revealed Colin.

That was not all. One of the gang knew how to put the pins back into hand grenades and another singed his eyebrows, eye lashes and hair while mixing up gunpowder.

Mavis related how they first met. It was rather romantic, being on Valentines Day in 1948.

"I was nearly 16 at the time and my older sister took me to the Winter Gardens dance. I couldn't dance but there were all these smashing young blokes and I sort of singled him out."

They were married in 1950 and ran their shop for over 40 years. Mavis had four children during this time and virtually never stopped working. When one of her children was born she was still in the shop until just before 5pm. Then it began to happen and en route to St Mary's Colin asked if she'd mind if he delivered the Whitwell grocery orders on the way. Mavis somehow held on and they made it.

In 1972, with their new business partners, Leon Simmonds and his wife Ann, they also took over Baverstock's, the other village grocery store. That thriving business is now run by their grandson.

Many will remember Colin and Mavis as a formidable combination in our local badminton scene. They had more tiffs playing as a doubles team than they ever did indoors. Colin captained the Niton club for around 30 years. They had a very cramped hall, which visiting teams found rather difficult. There was a little gamesmanship, too. Especially when Mavis wore her frilly panties. I was watching a game there one night when their old dog pushed open the door and walked across the court during a vital game.

I was actually at the Seaview Sports Club when Niton beat Yarmouth B 5-4 in the very long final of the Mallett Cup. I got into trouble when I got home at 1.30am.

Mavis also played in our famous Niton Dollies football team who, with our other ladies teams, raised a lot of money for local charities. Mavis was 36 when she played her first match.

I loved the story of the day Colin had to reprimand a member of staff. A little later she told him if he spoke to her like that again, he could stick the job. So, he told her to go. As she was about to leave the store she realised she still had her shop nylon overall on. Off it came to reveal her petticoat and panties. They all had the full treatment. Not in Niton, surely!

CHAPTER 7

Chris McDonald

AFTER MOVING to the Island in 1965, Chris McDonald became one of our most respected policeman. He worked at Newport, Ryde, Sandown and Shanklin and quickly made friends from all walks of life. These included fellow coppers, team mates in his various sporting pastimes, ex-criminals and informers. He joined the force as a beat bobby but was never really keen to progress through the ranks. For a while he did join the major crime squad but was far happier walking the streets.

I suppose to most of us he was a real old fashioned copper. Well respected, fair, easy to talk to and proud of his job. Chris went out of his way to help.

The very last time we ever met was virtually on the eve of his move to East Sussex. I wrote an article on him in *The Beacon* and was invited to his farewell party. For a few years Chris and his wife Sue had run a Sandown hotel, after he retired from the police in 1998. They left the Island to enjoy complete retirement but, sadly, Chris died much too soon.

During that final interview he gave me his views on the changing world of a policeman.

"In the early days of my career the general public had so much respect for the police and we took such a pride in our work. Now, in many cases, they are just in it for the money. They now tell you how many weeks or years they have left in the job. How can you get to talk to the public when you are driving around in cars all day?"

He readily admitted he could not become a politically correct PC. There were many times when they had to bend the rules to get results.

"We also had real fun with colleagues which was great for station morale but today those pranks wouldn't be tolerated."

On one occasion the sergeant had nailed up PC McDonald's locker with wood, as he arrived for a 6am start. Within a couple of hours Chris had borrowed some price cards from a garage and put them on his sergeant's car, parked outside of his home. There were a lot of door knocks for the bargain priced vehicle.

Once in Union Street, Ryde, Chris noticed a police car with the keys still in it – and quickly drove it back to the station. This all happened while his colleagues were looking at cameras in a shop window.

While in the major crime squad he commuted to the mainland every day to work on murders. Locally, he was heavily involved with the Island's 1973 drug bust and a member of the firearms unit.

One of his favourite stories was the robbery at the Avenue Road Post Office, in Sandown, when a Robin Reliant was used as the getaway car.

Chris was so proud of his wonderful father, Jack. I wrote about him in the *Weekly Post*. He was a professional footballer and in 1945 won a Wartime FA Cup Final medal with Chelsea – and scored in front of 100,000 people at Wembley.

I also loved it when Chris related his Simon Dee story.

"Simon Dee came to play cricket at Shanklin for the Lords Taverners. Our skipper, Bill Jenkins, was not too impressed when he arrived with two 15 year olds on his arm. I wasn't supposed to bowl – and certainly not fast. Jenks put me on as soon as he arrived at the wicket, with instructions to get him out and create a little pain. I hit him with a fast delivery (not intended, of course) and he went down in a heap. He didn't see the next two and the third knocked his stumps out."

CHAPTER 8

Cyril Daish

CYRIL DAISH has always blown his own trumpet with great vigour and when I interviewed him it had been 75 years non-stop. He would much rather blow on his horn than talk about himself. He turned me down a few times before he finally gave in, back in 2015. I think his wife, Janet, finally persuaded him. It should have happened many years earlier.

When Cyril was just 11, he swapped all his toys for a bugle. It was not a family treasure and his mother used to hide it. One summer he couldn't find it at all. It was in the cooker, which they didn't use at that time of the year.

He went to the Sandown Boys Brigade to practice his trumpet. Then he also enjoyed wartime sessions at the St Alban's Hall, Ventnor.

"We used to have to dodge the bombs that were aimed at the nearby radar station. One night the ceiling collapsed but we continued playing."

When VE Day came he joined in the celebrations but had a limited repertoire. He played *Your Are My Sunshine* 20 times. No-one worried, the war was over.

In early 1946 Cyril used to catch the train from Sandown to Bembridge to play at the Marine pub, near the station. This led to village hall dances with their four piece band. That comprised of Cyril on trumpet, Mick Wavell on tenor sax and clarinet, Bruce Sothcott on drums and Hugh Jeffrey on piano.

His musical life changed when he joined the Island's George Wilkinson Band, who were resident at the Ventnor Winter Gardens. That was the hey day of the venue and 500 arrived every Saturday night via coaches from all around the Island. Cyril was in his element, especially when they supported the visiting star bands of that time. These included Ted Heath, Eric Delaney and the Squadronaires.

"The best night I ever had was when Britain's top trumpeter, Kenny Baker, came with the Ted Heath Band. Backstage, in the interval, he played my trumpet and I played his."

When he formed his own Cyril Daish Band they enjoyed seasons at Pilgrim's Park, Thorness. Then they moved closer to home and spent 11 years at Sandown's Ocean Hotel. Cyril even asked for a rider. It wasn't champagne and caviar – just a fan and a pint of milk. On Friday nights he asked all the ladies to bring clean perfumed knickers for when he played the song about waving them in the air. Then he moved to the Trouville for 13 years and some of the guests from the Ocean still came to see him.

I can still remember the Godshill Cricket Club dances when the village hall shook to *My Ding-A-Ling*. Cyril had his own version of that Chuck Berry song.

In the early 70s, Cyril was lucky to survive a late night accident. On their way home from Pilgrim's Park they were hit by a drunk driver at Blackwater. The side of their car was sliced off and a hub cap came through the windscreen and the glass missed his eye by an inch. He needed 22 stitches.

At one time, movie director Herbert Wilcox was staying at the Ocean Hotel and was so impressed with Cyril. He even offered him an eight month cruise but he turned it down.

In the past few years he's been plagued by the trumpeter's curse, when the lip goes. It happened to the late Kenny Ball. It means Cyril can't play for so long or so loud. At least the trumpet is not still in the cooker!

CHAPTER 9

Den Clare

FOR SOME REASON it took me 21 years to finally interview Den Clare. His introduction took longer than some interviews. His life had included being an Island policeman, toy shop owner, hypnotherapist, a registered healer, advertising salesman, celebrity driver, property dealer, local councillor and cub leader. My biggest surprise was seeing him as the father of the bride in the final scene of *Reach For The Moon*, the television series filmed on the Island. Apparently it was 75 degrees in Yarmouth Church when it was filmed.

Den began life in what was one of the most safe jobs around. He found banking quite boring, despite doing well, and the day he was called into the manager's for his chat with the boss was to change his life for ever.

"He said to me 'Mr Clare you are doing well and by the time you are 40 you will be a bank manager.' I was young and thought whoever gets to 40, it's very old.

"I decided to leave there and then and gave in my notice. I saw an advert about joining the police and the station was right next door. I was accepted and joined the Hampshire and Isle of Wight force in Aldershot. After my training, I was posted to Shanklin."

Being a good looking young guy, he had young ladies pleading for him to arrest them. He often arranged to meet them when his duty ended. I'm going to leave it there.

He'd arrived in Shanklin in peak summer and was so busy as the area was full of holidaymakers. When it came to early morning winter patrols in the town, it was far less exciting.

Many remember him for Den's Toy Box in Regent Street. He'd eventually moved on from lonely nights walking the streets.

When he was just five, his sister had a really bad pain in her knee and Den put his hand on it and it went away. That could have well been the start of his healing capabilities. He later had a problem cured by a spiritual healer and that set him thinking. For many years Den has also been a successful hypnotherapist and was once called on by one of the world's most successful singer songwriters. *Fields Of Gold* and all that.

Den was a celebrity driver and arranger at many of our Music Festivals at Seaclose Park.

"I was first asked if I would like to drive a guy called Chris Martin. I'd never even heard of him. Then I was told he was from Coldplay. I enjoyed it and got to drive many of the stars who came. Then I was asked to arrange which drivers would pick up certain stars. I had a great conversation with Sting en route from his helicopter landing in Freshwater. I loved picking up Donovan from Gatwick. I met so many famous people like Paul McCartney and Tom Jones."

One of his hobbies is being photographed with famous people. He was desperate to meet Joe Brown. I knew Joe and went to ask him if he would be in a photograph with Den. Joe was not in the mood – but he did it on his next visit to the Island.

Den, who has five children and at least five grandchildren, loves family life with his lovely partner Elaine Caesar. His motto is life is all about enjoying yourself.

His favourite television series was *The Bill* and he once met a guy who wanted some help to become a hypnotherapist. He told Den he was a producer on *The Bill*. There was a happy ending and Den and Elaine were seen as extras in a pub scene with the character Tony Stamp. It took four hours and on screen it was all over in 20 seconds.

CHAPTER 10
Dave Cannon

I WAS ONE of the lucky ones who managed to get into the Hotel Ryde Castle function room in October 2018 to see Dave Cannon celebrate an incredible 50 years as an Island DJ. It was standing room only. It had all started, officially, in 1968 when the La Babalu resident DJ, Malc Lawrence, gave Dave the chance of a Tuesday rock 'n' roll nostalgia night at the club. Old pupils of Cowes Secondary Modern can go back even further than that. To 1962, in fact. On wet lunch breaks Dave would nip home to get his records to play in the main hall.

How times had changed. When he was at Ward Avenue he just had a handful of 45s. At the Ryde Castle he had over 30,000 to choose from, on MP3. That's not all. There were also 16,000 videos. Some of stars featured you can barely remember. Dave also has certain other artists singing some of the songs you wish you'd forgotten. He spends many tedious hours putting these together and they are brilliant. Somehow he manages to merge together records and live performances. Few would have his patience.

One summer night Dave invited me to watch his show at the Shanklin Beach Hotel. What an eye opener that was. The hotel guests chose the show. He asked them their favourite singers and almost before they could say Matt Monro or Frankie Laine, there they were on screen singing unforgettable hits.

Back in the 70s Dave was head hunted by Derek Hockley, who ran Solent City Sound, one of the early travelling discos. Derek was not a DJ but had built some amazing equipment. Together, they did gigs for £9 a night. Derek took £6 and Dave took the other three. When Derek decided to emigrate to Australia he offered Dave the whole set-up for just £100. This included the rights to the name, two speakers, all the records, a Morris 1000 van and a slide projector – and he didn't have to bid on eBay.

Dave bought many of his records from Lucky Dip, who were on Coppins Bridge before moving to opposite County Hall.

Sometimes in life you have to make brave decisions – and in 1979 Dave did just that. He left Clark Masts to, hopefully, become a full time DJ. He certainly made the right move. The *Ryde Queen* took him on as their resident DJ and maintenance man. He's never looked back. Now it might be difficult to go back there for a rusty reunion gig! He does perform about 50 yards away at The Breeze.

Dave Cannon is not just a DJ who throws the kit into a van and just turns up at the gig. He plans his nights and is always prepared to keep up to date with modern technology. Every time I go to his house he proudly shows me a new gadget. One of these can get thousands of internet radio stations, with real caring presenters, going back to the glory days of the wireless, when they more interested in the music than themselves.

Over the years Dave has raised thousands of pounds for local charities, particularly the EM Hospice. In 1995 his La Babalu reunion night raised over £1000 for the hospice.

Dave has recovered from cancer and another life threatening illness. In 1999 he was such an inspiration to many people.

"I was determined to beat cancer and kept working to take my mind off the illness. After my treatment I did catch an infection and spent four weeks in a St Mary's isolation ward," said Dave.

At his 2018 celebration it was so wonderful to see Malc Lawrence join him on stage, despite being unwell. It was all down to you Malc.

CHAPTER 11

Jeremy Short

WHEN I WAS QUITE young my father, who had been an active rider for the Vectis Roads Cycling Club, still took a great interest in the local club and we would go to Cowes Recreation Ground to see the start of the club's early Sunday morning 25 mile time trials. I seem to remember a guy called Pete Brown as their star rider of the time. As they arrived back, there was always the dream of sub-60 minute 25 mile – but it never happened until around 30 years later. Then a 17 year old junior called Jeremy Short clocked under 59 minutes and eventually smashed every club record.

Back in 2013 I wrote an article on him in *The Beacon* and many customers of his famous local fencing business were unaware that he was in fact the Island's cycling legend. That year he also made a return visit to my radio show.

How times had changed in the world of cycling. When Jeremy's father bought him his first racing bike it cost £55. At the time of our interview Bradley Wiggins model that he won the Tour de France with would have been not far off £15,000. When Jeremy was at the peak of his own racing career he was riding a £700 machine.

His father was such an influence on him – despite being so tough with Jerry's training schedules.

"My father set up a nine-mile course from Blackgang to Compton Bay. If my speed dropped below 30mph he would honk the car horn at me. It was tough but worth it in the end."

Jeremy broke every Vectis Roads record at both junior and senior level. In 1980, on a Raleigh TI aluminium bike, with spoke wheels, he recorded an amazing 1 hour 58 minutes for a 50 mile event. With today's modern bikes and equipment he would have knocked a minute or two off that incredible time.

He was the Island's top all-round rider for six years in a row. To improve on his times, even more, he needed to move to a top mainland club. That led to him joining the Antelope Racing Club, where he became the South of England's top all-round rider and also won national medals. In 1992 he beat several top British riders. He remained a second claim rider for the Vectis Roads.

After a fantastic 1992 season, when he was a feared rider, Jeremy took a break from competitive cycling. He had a niggling injury, family commitments and was building up his own fencing business.

A few years later he went back to cycling, as a kind of therapy to help him deal with so many setbacks. He lost his mother, his marriage broke up and he had two boys to bring up as a single parent. Also he was suffering from an eating disorder. Amazingly, he still broke records and set some incredible times as a Vectis Roads veteran, including 54 minutes for a 25 mile race.

Jeremy kept his bulimia illness very quiet and even won the team event, with Jack Grundy, in the 2003 West Wight Triathlon.

These days he's getting his life back on track and still cycles to keep fit and is often joined by his six-year old daughter Poppy, the light of his life, who manages around six miles. He also does a Park Run once a week and Poppy does the junior event.

On the way home from our last interview I thought of Jeremy for nine miles – as I drove along his old Military Road training course. No, not on my bike – I haven't ridden one for 50 years.

CHAPTER 12

Ian Mac

I INVITED IAN MAC on to my radio show just after he'd been voted the most popular presenter on IW Radio. It seemed perfectly timed and he was very modest about the poll and was just grateful and surprised to have won it. As well as being a natural broadcaster, Ian was so good at live gigs and could easily whip up an audience in no time.

He grew up on Pan Estate and was very proud of that fact.

"I think people have lumbered us with different stigmas. It's totally unfair. I lived there for 20 years and the whole time it was a really nice place to grow up in. I can never remember there being masses of trouble."

He loved radio DJs like Tom Browne, Dave Lee Travis and Tony Blackburn and had a dream of playing records to the public. These days he's gone way beyond that and now runs his own radio station, Vectis Radio. That took some courage and he finally got his licence for FM transmissions.

On his own admission, he was not a good boat builder. He joined on a YTS scheme and got £23-50 a week. It was not a red letter day when he started – although red did come into it rather quickly. Early on, he was asked to paint red lead on the inside of a boat and thought he'd done a job that Rembrandt would have been proud of. The boss was not so impressed and sacked him.

"I left on the Friday but went back to him on the Monday morning with my certificate to say I was colour blind, so he had to take me back on."

Ian worked at Plessey Radar after this but finally left to become a full time DJ. He suddenly was offered a ten week contract in Egypt but his mates advised him not to go, as it might be rather a culture shock.

He lived like a king for the first few weeks in the large hotel, as their club DJ. Then it all changed.

"When I was nearing the end of my contract they wouldn't tell me where I was going to go. I knew that Ramadan was coming up and they were going to redo the club and open it up with a new DJ. So I decided I was going to go home, as they had not promised me anything. They told me if I left, all the things in my contract were null and void. I was later called into the office and told I owed them £1500 for my keep, food and drinks. I had about £20 at the time. They called in two policemen with guns. I thought there was going to be an international incident.

"Luckily a guy I knew who had worked in the hotel managed to get me a flight but I would have to sneak out. He came at 7am in the morning with a wheelie linen bin and told me to get in there with my suitcases. I went out the fire exit and there was a car waiting to take me to the airport. It was scary."

Ian also revealed that when he was 20 years old his mother told him that his dad was not his real dad. She was quite happy for him to try and track him down but it proved impossible as the names were different. Thanks to a listener's skill on the internet, some 18 years later he finally tracked down his dad. What a happy ending! Ian's parents met up again, fell in love and got married. The best man was their 38 year old son.

In his wedding speech he brought the house down by saying he was now finally no longer a b-----d.

PS. Ian, I'm still available for an interview.

CHAPTER 13

Jeremy Irons
The Isle of Wight Years

JEREMY IRONS is the most successful Island-born actor of all time. He's made over 50 movies including some huge box-office hits like *The Mission, Lolita, Die Hard With A Vengeance, Reversal Of Fortune, The French Lieutenant's Woman* and the huge television series *Brideshead Revisited*. Quite an achievement for a young kid who grew up in St Helens.

I've been lucky enough to have interviewed him on two occasions and was completely fascinated by his memories of growing up on the Island. I was born in East Cowes and can still remember seeing the name of P D Irons on the vans and lorries of aircraft makers Saunders-Roe. For a while he was their company secretary. That was his father, Paul.

Jeremy was actually born in a Cowes nursing home but was quickly whisked off to St Helens the very next day. He's always been so proud of his Island roots.

"Being born on an island, off an island, is great and you can't get more insular than that. I had such a happy childhood on the Isle of Wight."

He could still remember his father being a founder member of Brading Haven Yacht Club, where he owned a Solent scow.

"I can still vividly see my father sitting in the bottom of a scow, sideways, with his feet lolling over the edge. With not enough wind to take him out of St Helens Harbour he could be seen drifting slowly backwards, smoking through his long cigarette holder, without a care in the world."

Jeremy loved the rivalry between his village and nearby Bembridge, particularly within the sailing clubs. He was also most keen to point out, with a glint in his eye, that it is really St Helens Harbour and not Bembridge Harbour, as some neighbours often call it.

He told me this during our first interview, at the Royal Shakespeare Theatre, Stratford. "All the knobs were members of the Bembridge Sailing Club and the proper sailors, who liked a bit of fun, were at Brading Haven."

His first school was actually in enemy territory. It was Greylands in Bembridge. That daily trip was via a steam train from St Helens to Bembridge. He can still remember that turntable at the end of the line. Back at St Helens he was always met by the nanny, who even taught him his alphabet, backwards.

The Irons family home overlooked the harbour, which could be reached through a small wood at the bottom of the garden. Jeremy enjoyed that idyllic setting. He also could be seen walking their two dogs around the green. He once told me some of his family were interested in buying the family home. It's rather different now!

Amazingly, Jeremy later went as a boarder to a public school at Appley. He felt it was far too early, as he was only aged seven. At least he made his acting debut at that now defunct Ryde school. He played a Miss Marple-type character with a tweed jacket and skirt, wig and high heels. What would Simon Gruber have made of it?

Jeremy's other special memories of the Island include afternoon tea at the famous Galleon Restaurant in Ryde, where he often asked the band to play *The Teddy Bears Picnic*, and riding the family ponies across the downs.

Dennis Danby, a Bembridge veterinary surgeon, was an early mentor for young Jeremy and it was no surprise his initial dream was to be a vet.

In the mid-80s Jeremy and his wife, actor Sinead Cusack, sailed to the Island in an Enterprise dingy and illegally landed for a picnic at Osborne House. A few years later it was in a powerboat to lunch with his sister in Seaview.

CHAPTER 14

Peter Boffin

I STILL GET EXCITED when I see the name of Peter Boffin appear on the closing credits of numerous re-runs of old hit television series. They were huge shows, too. *Man About The House*, *George And Mildred* and *Fresh Fields* were watched by millions. *George And Mildred* was a number one hit – and starred Ventnor-born Brian Murphy. Peter was their vision mixer

Peter and his wife, Rita, moved to Niton to kind of retire but it never happened quite like that. He acted in plays for the Apollo and Pepperpot Players, was a familiar voice to our blind community, via reading the *County Press* on cassettes and then memory sticks. He was also involved with two Island television stations, TV 12 and Solent TV, made videos for Blackgang Chine and many remember his animated scenery, projected on screen, for the Apollo's *The Lion, The Witch And The Wardrobe*. Peter also produced a few unexpected laughs – when he forgot his lines.

I'll never forget seeing him playing the seedy old photographer, Monsieur Bourgeron Couchon, in *Gypsy*, at the Apollo. I gave him a wide berth for a little while!! Scary or what?

Peter would never invent the names of top stars he'd worked with. His successful career in top class television included working on shows with Morecambe and Wise, Tommy Cooper, Benny Hill and Zippy, George and Bungle. I put this to the test on one occasion, when I interviewed Tommy Steele. The legendary entertainer got quite excited when I asked him about Peter Boffin. Peter had told me he had worked on Tommy's hit shows like *Quincey's Quest*, which won a BAFTA Craft Award, and *Tommy Steele And A Show.*

Peter once told me, during one of our interviews: "Tommy was so great to work with and very professional. On one occasion there were six of us, including him, having lunch in the studio canteen and he said he would pay for all of us. Those were the days – and he even got change from his fiver."

Early in Peter's career, when he was working for Kodak, he was tempted by a newspaper advert from ITV, who were looking for television cameramen. It had caught his eye and a few thousand others. He didn't' make it but was rather clever. His letter to the BBC must have impressed their studio bosses, as they had lost so many cameramen to the new ITV set up, at twice the money.

"I struck lucky as it was six months before ITV went on air. By that time I'd gained a lot of experience."

He worked on huge shows like *The Grove Family*, *Six-Five Special*, *Whack-O!*, with Jimmy Edwards, and *Whirligig*. On one, called *The River Line*, Peter was steering a camera on a huge crane and got into the wrong position and almost demolished the set. Amazingly, shortly after this he was promoted to vision mixer.

In time, he left the BBC for more money at Associated Rediffusion, which was a London area ITV station. They provided much of the nationwide output. During his 30 years with them and later Thames Television he worked on some memorable shows. These included *Morecambe And Wise*, *Callan*, *Tommy Cooper* and *Rainbow*.

In the latter days of his career he became freelance. His last show, before coming to the Island, was *Best Of Friends*, with Sir John Gielgud, Patrick McGoohan and Wendy Hiller.

What is a vision mixer? Peter explained it to me. "I sat next to the director as a kind of film editor. I would be looking at images from three or four cameras and instantly choose the on-screen shots and edited them as the show rolled. Special effects and captions were other key elements."

CHAPTER 15

Cyril Caplehorn

IN 2009 I HEADED to Newport's Cornelia Manor care home to interview a very special resident. I hadn't seen him for 30 years and he still looked so good and, as ever, was full of fun. Cyril Caplehorn was actually 100 that very day. He'd never had a serious illness in his life and was as chirpy as ever. He had a remarkable memory and could even still remember the First World War.

His family lived in Lugley Street, Newport, and the front door opened straight on to the pavement. It was never locked at all until they went to bed. If they went out, they would simply leave the house unlocked.

Cyril was always good at spelling. At school he had to be. If the teacher saw a word spelt wrongly, it was a cane across the knuckles.

"I think we benefitted from our teachers being so strict. We grew up to respect discipline and were all the better for it."

On Sundays it was Sunday school in the morning and afternoon and also two church services. His best clothes, including a stiff collar, were taken out of the wardrobe. Newport was almost like a ghost town. Not a single shop was open.

Cyril barely ever went out of Newport. A special treat was to catch the steam train to Wootton and then walk to Woodside Bay for a swim. Their other entertainment was playing games in the Petticoat Lane fields. Did the boys chase the girls?

"Oh yes, we used to chase the girls alright. I could name one or two but I'd better not," said Cyril, with a glint in his eye. I did suggest to him that it was probably a bit too late to worry about that.

Luckily, Cyril found the girl of his dreams and they were happily married for many years and did celebrate their golden wedding. When they first got married Cyril was getting the equivalent of £3.25 a week. They somehow managed and in those days wives never went out to work.

Cyril joined Roach Pittis, the solicitors, on October 1, 1923, and stayed until he retired at 65. Then he went back part-time until he was 80. For many years he specialised in divorces and with no divorce court here on the Island they had to go to Southampton.

"When I joined Roach Pittis, at the age of 14, I was told by Mr Palmer, the principal, that I would see and hear a lot of confidential things going on in the office. If I discussed any of these I would be instantly dismissed."

Cyril loved his football and supported Newport and Southampton. He could remember Newport taking 11 full coaches of supporters to an away FA Cup first round tie at Swindon Town. They lost by the odd goal. On another trip to Hinckley Athletic, the coaches got back at 8am the next morning.

He loved telling stories. Many was the time I saw him revealing a yarn to a few eager listeners. You rarely saw Cyril without a smile on his face. His love for life and people must have helped him live for such a long time.

When he was 97, Cyril was invited to the Exeter wedding of his granddaughter. He said he would only go if he could travel there and back in the same day. Then he got a shock. A helicopter was booked from Newport football ground to Exeter. He needed a carer from the home to go with him and that was no problem. They left the ground at 11.40am and were in Exeter in just over an hour. They went to the 2pm wedding and the reception and then flew back to Newport at 7.30pm.

CHAPTER 16

Dave Woodford

WHEN DAVE WOODFORD was a Niton teenager his driving skills were not always appreciated by the villagers. Most of the time he only had two of his four wheels on the ground. When I first met him, for the past 30 years he'd become a much respected lorry driver.

I knew his lovely wife Mary and between us we talked him into appearing live on my radio show. He was such a hit and came back at least three more times. Before the broadcast I went to their home to plan the programme. Unfortunately, I forgot my

gasmask. It was long after the war but they were both heavy smokers and it was hard to breath. When I got home I was told to put all my clothes on the washing line for a fresh air blow out.

In the early days it was tough to drive to Yorkshire and Scotland. Some nights he slept in the cab and tried to ignore the ice on the inside of the windscreen. He put a makeshift bed across the seats and the hump in the middle played havoc with his back. For warmth he would jump out of the cab and stand around the exhaust. Many years later his Vectis Transport lorry had a sleeping compartment, night heater and television.

His longest ever Island trip was the day it took him ten hours to deliver a lorry load of hay from Wellow to St Helens. It was an eventful journey that included replacing a steering box, unloading part of the hay in Pyle Street to get the lorry into Canning Day's repair shop and, much later in the day, making the mistake of going into the Vine Inn to find out the way to the address.

"I should have visited Mary, who'd just had our first baby in St Mary's. I never did get there and she's never let me forget it," revealed Dave.

On one horrendous occasion Dave had a lucky escape on the M1. His huge lorry had a tyre blow out and careered across the lanes and hit the crash barrier, which cut his air supply to the brakes and it was some time before he stopped.

"The police asked me if I would like to walk back and see how far I'd gone along the barrier. It seemed like walking from Newport to Niton.

"I was so frightened I was going to cross into the south bound carriageway and hit other traffic. I could have killed a dozen people."

Dave and his pals always had a few tricks up their sleeves until the tougher regulations come in with the birth of tachographs, timed deliveries and other modern aids.

On one memorable Sunday I had three wonderful lorry drivers live on the same show. Dave, Sid West and Geoff Reynolds. People still talk about it.

Dave told us all a great story of a new lorry drivers motel near Perth in Scotland

"Three of us drivers were each taking a full load of Island potatoes from Jim Flux at Godshill. We all met up at this new motel. One of the lads had his wife with him, so we booked in four drivers and smuggled her in. A lady ran this place and there was a rule no women were allowed in the rooms. They had double bunks and I was sharing with the other driver. Suddenly the door opened and this manageress was there with this security bloke. She said to me: 'We're looking for a woman. Have you got one in here?' I said, no, I've been looking for one myself all evening but can't find one!"

Apparently the driver and his wife had to spend the night in the cab. They would not believe she was his wife.

CHAPTER 17

Pete Hogman

BACK IN 1987 Pete Hogan and his delightful wife, Gilly, moved to the Island to relax a little more and get away from seven nights a week gigging with their Hoggie's Jump Band. Although he quietly slipped into Bembridge, his musical story was rather spectacular. His career path had included Rod Stewart, Jimmy Powell and the Five Dimensions, Millie, PJ Proby, Chuck Berry and TV shows like *Ready Steady Go* and *Thank Your Lucky Stars*.

I feel so fortunate to have interviewed him on several occasions, for both radio and local newspapers. He had such a fund of stories and was one of thousands of young British guys influenced by Lonnie Donegan and the rise of skiffle.

On one occasion he came on my radio show, with Brian Sharpe, to celebrate the first album from Hoggie and the Sharpetones, such a popular local live band. Ironically, it came out 40 years after Pete had first visited the Island. On that trip the only music played would probably have been a bugle. He was with a London Boys Brigade company, who camped at Fort Albert, near Yarmouth.

Some musical myths are completely groundless. One of these was the fact that Rod Stewart had played harmonica on Millie's *My Boy Lollipop*. There was not a note of truth in it. It was, in fact, Pete Hogman and he got £7.50 for the session. However, he did owe Rod something of a debt.

He told me this during our first ever interview, back in 1989. "I was on a Ban The Bomb march and this guy came up to me and said I was not bad on harmonica. It was Rod Stewart. He told me he was leaving the band he was in, Jimmy Powell and the Five Dimensions, to join Long John Baldry. He told me I should attend the audition for his job. I went to the Railway Hotel, Harrow and got it, after sitting in for one number. Suddenly I was on the road as a professional musician."

For a while he also became a session musician and, as well as playing on Millie's record, he also played harmonica on PJ Proby's *Hold Me*. That time his fee rose to £25. Also on that Proby session was Big Jim Sullivan and an unknown Jimmy Page.

I loved his Chuck Berry story. He became the only British harmonica player to appear on a Chuck Berry track. They recorded an album called *Chuck Berry In England*. Pete was in the backing band for that tour of Britain in 1965.

"Chuck was such a nice guy and offered to give us a song for nothing for the Five Dimensions. Jimmy had left by then and I did more of the singing. When his sister found out about the song she wanted £500 for it. We couldn't afford it. The song was called *No Particular Place To Go*."

"He asked me to go back to the States with him. I didn't like flying at the time and turned him down. I now realise I shouldn't have done that. Mind you, I wouldn't have met my lovely wife Gill, if I had."

After settling on the Island, Pete, a great artist, taught art and crafts in Parkhurst Prison. He sometimes took in his band. At one time, when it was a Category A prison, they formed their own group. Before moving to the Island he was a prop maker at Pinewood and Borehamwood studios for movies, early pop videos and training films.

It was such a sad loss when Pete died in December 2017. In November 2018 there was a brilliant gig to celebrate his life and music.

CHAPTER 18

Jennie Linden

OVER THE PAST 45 years I have been so lucky with huge scoops for the *Weekly Post*, IW *Radio* and the *County Press*. I had no real problem losing out on the news that movie star Jennie Linden was now living on the Island and doing talks about her career. In fact, my good friend Jon Moreno from the CP beat me to it and almost had a weekly column on her local activities. I bided my time and then caught up with her in Bembridge and, apparently, surprised her with my research.

Jennie and her husband, Chris, had been regular summer visitors to Seaview in their younger days. Many years later when a friend sent them a postcard of a painting of the village they decided they would retire there. They could not find a property that suited them but found the perfect home in nearby Bembridge.

I knew many people still wanted to talk to Jennie about the nude wrestling scene in *Women In Love*, the international movie she made with Alan Bates, Oliver Reed and Glenda Jackson. I decided to wait a while before we got around to that.

Jennie's parents, like many others over the years, tried to talk their daughter out of going to drama school. They would only let her go to London's Central School if she studied to be a drama teacher. During those three years she had continual disappointments.

"I wanted to be an actor and I could look through glass and see people like Julie Christie, Lynn Redgrave, Judi Dench and Vanessa Redgrave doing what I wanted to do. There was I having to read books on literature," said Jennie.

When she left she managed to go straight into repertory in Wolverhampton and then joined Ian McKellen's company in Coventry. She then obtained a few early television

spots in *Emergency Ward 10*, *The Avengers* and *Armchair Theatre*, followed by two memorable appearances in *The Saint*, with Roger Moore.

"I was very excited. He was ridiculously beautiful and later when I was in the South of France filming *The Persuaders*, with Tony Curtis and him, I think he was at the peak of his good looks. He was so funny to be with and was always up to tricks.

"Apparently, when he was filming the Bond movie *Moonraker* they had to shoot a scene inside the rocket, when they would be thousands of miles into space. When the camera panned to the window there was a props man cleaning it with a cloth. Roger set that up and got told off."

Did Jennie turn down the movie *Straw Dogs*? "Yes I did and I'm so glad I chose not to do it. I also turned down *The Nightcomers* with Marlon Brando. In both those movies the women had no real character to them. They were just there to be used. I didn't want that."

I've always felt *Women In Love* was over-hyped because of the nude wrestling scene. I was keen to find out her view.

"That was certain to get all the publicity. It was remarkable at the time but there were other things in that movie that got overshadowed by all the publicity. Ken Russell did some amazing things in the way that movie was shot."

Jennie then lost out to Julie Christie for the lead in *The Go Between* but signed to appear in *Severed Head*, with Richard Attenborough. She felt the movie never worked and the characters just didn't gel. The movie makers wanted her to move to America but with a young child at home, neither Jennie or her husband wanted to go down that road.

She remained busy in Britain with television, movie and stage work. She retired in the late 80s and trained as a reflexologist.

I love meeting up with her and she is a credit to the entertainment industry.

CHAPTER 19

Fred Sage

IN 1946 FRED SAGE came to the Island from London with a vision for post-war tenting holidays and he bought a field and a bungalow at Thorness Bay for £2000. By the 70s he'd built up quite an empire until a Jersey bank, which was in financial trouble, called in his £500,000 loan overnight and, after a valiant fight, he had to concede and end any more dreams for The Towers and Pilgrim's holiday centres.

I'd known of Fred for many years but didn't really get to know him until 2000, when I managed to tempt him on to my IW *Radio* chat show. I admired Fred for being brave enough to even come on the show, as he'd always had a speech impediment. It all worked out well and in 2010 part of that interview was actually released on one of my CDs, called *Gone But Not Forgotten*, which featured past Islanders with wonderful stories. Sadly, Fred had passed away by then.

When I first interviewed him he was 88 and certainly up for it. Amazingly, he had no real regrets and maintained that cheery disposition that had seen him through a few crises. He told me: "When I lost everything I just felt annoyed as it was so unjustified."

Born in Bow, Fred worked in a Camden Town tobacco factory for 15 years but never smoked throughout his life. He didn't drink alcohol, either. At Thorness Bay he wouldn't have had time anyway. He worked 18 hours a day.

During the war Fred, who had been working as an engineer for the Stratford Co-op in East London, bought three lorries and made a living delivering hardcore and sand to the many aerodromes that were being built. Twenty years on, he ran Sage Construction on the Island and employed 100 men.

After the war he came to Thorness with his two brothers, Frank and Lou, after seeing the land advertised in *Dalton's Weekly*. Following the success of the tenting field he bought Towers House and turned it into a guest house.

"I had a few encounters with the planning authorities but eventually was allowed to put caravans on my site."

At that time the Cowes Council was about to demolish the town's pier and was open to reasonable offers. Fred, somewhat tongue-in-cheek, offered £50 for the wooden pavilion building. They told him if he paid £100, within a month, he could take it away. That was quickly a done deal. Fred used most of the wood to build caravans in an old stable at Osborne.

The Towers complex, as basic as it was, became very successful. One night they did have a problem when the dance floor caved in. It was built over a cellar. The dancers were back the following night.

The Towers also had the Island's first indoor swimming pool and many new chalets. In peak season there were over 1000 on site. In winter they let local swimming clubs use the pool facilities.

Fred eventually bought the nearby Pilgrim's Park Holiday Centre and made it into one huge complex. Years later Bourne Leisure bought the complete complex.

At the 1970 Pop Festival Fred provided caravans for the stars like Jimi Hendrix and Joan Baez.

Fred was happiest when working alongside his staff and this continued when he formed Sage Construction. This company was created to allow his men to work though the winter as well. Many of his holiday camp workers became skilled craftsmen. His company built hundreds of homes in Gurnard and Northwood.

The last thing Fred ever said to me was: "I wouldn't really change anything. I've never made a fortune but I've been happy – and that is much more important."

CHAPTER 20

Derek Ohren

I COULD WRITE a few chapters on Derek Ohren's life in Island football, as both a player and very successful manager. I've interviewed him for the *Weekly Post*, IW *Radio*, TV12 and *The Beacon*. I love his sense of fun and ready wit – with or without his teeth in!

We have had some great fun over the years and Derek has come through one or two shocks to enjoy life to the full. He was born with a heart defect and was lucky to play

football as long as he did. During the latter stages of his playing career he could have collapsed at any time. In his younger days, when he was working for a meat company, his arm was severely damaged by a lorry backing in. It crushed his arm and severed an artery. The hospital took a vein from his leg and put it in his arm.

When Derek first joined the Post Office you could get away with a lot more than you can today. Early on, one of his workmates asked him to help deliver a couple of fridges. They hadn't arrived by parcel post – and one was just dropped off at the tip. Then he realised it wasn't a work job. Nor was the day they took a new company van to move some hot manure. It was not bagged, either. The poor postman who drove the van the next morning had quite a shock when he opened the door. It created a big stink – in more ways than one!

On or off the football field Derek was not a fast mover. Once a local paper headline stated "Go Slow Derek Signs For Newport." One day he was a wee bit embarrassed. On his post round he was chased by a dog, which overtook him. Then he suddenly realised it only had three legs.

Our Derek was one of the first footballers ever to wear coloured boots. He'd been given a bright green pair to try out when he played for East Cowes Vics in a game at Christchurch. He never put a foot right in the first half and in the interval was told by manager Graham Daish to change back to his old ones.

Teeth have been the bane of his life. When he was a teenager playing for Newport's first team he niggled the opposition goalkeeper and minutes later the keeper punched his teeth and not the ball – and a few lost their roots.

When his workmates got a pay rise, with back pay, they went to Booker T's to celebrate. After about five hours Derek went to the toilet, as he felt unwell. He was so sick that his teeth came out as well – and he never saw them again. He barely said a word for two weeks until his new dentures arrived.

For six years he had his own Nighthawk Disco and was a regular at Newport Football Club and in summer at a Whitecliff Bay holiday park. Sometimes he left Bembridge and went straight to work and just sat in his van outside, ready for the early start. On some football Saturdays he worked from 5am until 9, then went coaching young footballers until 11.30. Then often dashed off to the mainland to play football. He'd get back home and sleep through *Match Of The Day*.

Derek never liked refusing to sign for any club. Once at Seaclose all the five Sunday League clubs he'd signed for all asked him to play for them. He did get into a little bother.

He is a fun guy but, in a more serious vein, has worked wonders with his coaching skills for so many young Island schoolboy footballers. He's also done such a lot for local charities. He also took Cowes Sports to new cup heights when he managed them for many seasons.

CHAPTER 21

David & Jenny Ball

I FIRST MET David and Jenny Ball back in 1960. I was playing cricket for Northwood 2nd XI, alongside the likes of Joe Marshall, 'Slim' Morris, Graham Rashley and the Calloway brothers. David had come to work at County Hall and joined us for a few games. He looked a very useful seam bowler and the following season took a 100 wickets. Jenny became a volunteer tea lady. Another very welcome acquisition.

David went on to become the club secretary and captained the second XI for a few seasons. They quickly became such popular characters at the cricket club.

Now when I see them briskly walking up Newport's St Johns Road, with a couple of shopping bags, I marvel at what they have both achieved in Island sport. David loved playing his rugby and eventually became a much sought after coach. Then he became so heavily involved with the Inter Island Games and helped to take our local sport to a higher level. Jenny, along with Darren Mew, has done so much for Island swimming. She has also found world swimming fame with some amazing performances in Masters events.

They are such an inspirational couple and simply refuse to grow old. Jenny is still swimming competitively and is so keen to encourage others to try the sport. She was in her 50s before she took up competition swimming. Over the years she's won so many medals but openly admits she is not that interested in winning them. She has swum all around the world, from London's Serpentine to the open sea around Lanzarote and has completed at least six cross-Solent swims. Her grandchildren love to go swimming with grandma when they come here for holidays.

It was just as well that Jenny was once a nurse. Her husband has been rather injury prone. You may just wince at a few of these. In one rugby match at Portchester he had ten teeth removed, without gas or anaesthetic. All it took was an opponent's boot. Cap that – and he can. During his luckless career he has broken his nose six times, had 11 stitches in a lip injury and broken a shoulder blade.

"Once when I was playing in a local derby against the Hurricanes I split my forehead. When I arrived in the hospital waiting room the other people were horrified when my blood-stained figure came through the door. Apparently, I kept saying there were 20 minutes left and could I go back to the match," revealed David.

During a match in Jersey he suffered a serious nose injury, which was strapped up for the return home. Some of his team mates tipped off the custom officials that he really had a watch strapped to his nose. They were not amused and put him through the x-ray machine, only to find it was a stitch-up, in more ways than one.

David played rugby for the IW RFC from 1961 to 1983. Later he became involved with a very successful Ventnor team. In one epic season they amassed 690 points, an average of 43 a game. They beat Portsmouth Nomads 114-0. They won the Hampshire Division 2 title and the Hampshire Plate.

Jenny, who has set world records, loves a challenge. She's achieved some remarkable performances and has won gold, silver and bronze in competitions all around the world. She is also very modest and often you have to prise out her numerous achievements.

This delightful couple have given so much of their time to encourage sport here on the Island. I've always wanted to see them reverse roles. It's much too late now to see Jenny playing in a rugby scrum and David swimming for gold in the Masters.

CHAPTER 22

Dominic Minghella

IN OCTOBER 2018 Island-born Dominic Minghella proved just how much he loved his birthplace. He flew home from America just for an appearance at the IW Literary Festival. It proved well justified because he filled the marquee and was certainly a hit with the large audience. I was honoured to interview him on stage. What the audience didn't know was that he'd arrived just under an hour before his appearance, with no set plan for his hour-long session. I'd anticipated this and he was relieved. I also made him a promise that he would be in this book. I'm not sure he believed me.

Dominic, who was inspired by his late Oscar-winning brother Anthony, has very much made his own niche in the world of scriptwriting. Being the youngest of the five talented children born to Eddie and Gloria Minghella, he was aware he had hard acts to follow. On his first day at Medina High School he was asked by a teacher: "I bet you're not as bright as your sister." Thankfully, that was way off beam and a few years later he was studying at Oxford.

His Oxford pals thought he might end up in the world of commerce and big business. That was not his wish and the world of screenwriting seemed much more to his liking. After working for a company making TV commercials he found it far too aggressive. Despite nearly giving up the idea he eventually met television producer Deirdre Keir and his life was to change for ever. He worked with her on the BBC television series *Hamish MacBeth*. It was in the dual role of episode writer and script editor.

When he was commissioned by Martin Clunes to write the series *Doc Martin*, based on a character from the movie *Saving Grace*, it became a huge hit on mainstream television and the first season was watched by nine million people – and it was to grow even more in the following series. It was one of the most talked-about TV shows in Britain. Since then there have been spin-off series in several countries. Creating this worldwide hit show has proved such a milestone in his career. Even now he gets invites to countries like Australia where it has a huge following.

A year or two ago he was working in America and met a guy who had an ambition to move to England. In particular, Cornwall and the town where they filmed the TV series *Doc Martin*. He had such a shock when Dominic told him he'd created the series.

Dominic also created the BBC's 2006 production of *Robin Hood* and he went on to write 39 episodes. It instantly won more viewers that its ITV same-time opposition, *The Ant and Dec Show*. The series was filmed in Budapest.

He was offered work in America and was involved with the series called *Knightfall*, set in France with a theme of 14th century knights. He worked on at least ten episodes. This has also been seen on the History Channel.

He has hailed me as the greatest fan of the TV movie *The Scapegoat*, made under the banner of Island Films, set up with his partner Sarah Beardsall. It was premiered at the Medina Theatre, Newport. It also led me to interviewing one of the stars who attended, Sheridan Smith. At the time of writing this chapter I've seen it 14 times. By the time you read this it might well be up to 20.

The last time we met I surprised him by revealing his teenage acting debut to the live audience. It was in Anthony's first low budget short movie, *A Little Like Drowning*, filmed on the Island in 1977. He played Martino and the shoot took 15 days.

CHAPTER 23

Gil Taylor

WHEN I DISCOVERED that world famous cinematographer Gil Taylor was living just two miles from me it was a dream come true. His 50 movie credits included *Frenzy*, *A Hard Day's Night*, *The Omen*, *Escape To Athena* and *Star Wars*. Would he appear on my radio show? I spent an evening at his Arreton home and we became friends from then on. I also had a complete surprise when he showed me some of his fantastic paintings.

I had an idea to surprise him on the day of his live broadcast and it worked perfectly. Ryde-based movie actor Michael Sheard, who had worked with Gil on several movies, walked in to surprise him in the final few minutes of the programme.

Initially, the plan had been for Gil to become an architect. In that job he would never have worked with Gregory Peck, Roger Moore, Lee Remick, Harrison Ford, the Beatles or Tony Hancock – to name but a few.

During the war Gil's camera talents were appreciated by Winston Churchill and he undertook several important assignments. He vividly remembered going to film the German concentration camps at the end of the war. He visited both Auschwitz and Belsen

I wanted to know about Alfred Hitchcock who chose Gil as his cinematographer for *Frenzy*.

"I'd first worked for him in 1931 on a movie called *Number Seventeen*. I was a very junior person at the time and he promoted me very quickly to be the first assistant to his cameraman.

"He always played tricks on people. Like putting ex-lax in the coffee, handcuffing props and locking toilet doors when people were in a hurry. He also cut people's ties off. One day we managed to get him into the dark room and I cut off his tie. He was angry and said he would fire whoever did it. I got away with it. When he chose me for *Frenzy*, I did admit I was the culprit on that earlier movie."

On *The Omen* he loved working with Gregory Peck and Lee Remick. Gil also had his eye on one of the very expensive sports jackets that Peck wore in the movie. He was hoping to get one at the end of the shoot. He was surprised when the Hollywood legend took everything away with him, even the socks.

Gil was a Beatles fan and loved making *A Hard Day's Night* for Dick Lester. He recalled the Fab Four were like a chain gang and went everywhere together. They also loved their cheese rolls and jam butties.

I was also intrigued to find out whether Peter Sellers had a problem remembering his lines. It had always been rumoured

"I worked on *Dr Strangelove* and he certainly did on that movie. He had idiot boards about four feet by three feet behind the camera. He was a bit depressed at the time. Later I met him on another movie and he was so pleased to see me."

I had been warned not to talk about George Lucas, with regard to *Star Wars*.

Did Gil think it would become an epic?

"It's become one but I never expected that when I first took on the assignment and nor did anyone else. I also had a lot to do with the lighting and it was my idea that helped to create the laser swords."

Other memories were going to Tony Hancock's private parties and he became very close to the legendary comic, having worked on *The Rebel* and *The Punch And Judy Man*.

I was flattered to be invited to one of Gils's small intimate dinner parties, hosted by his delightful wife Dee, who also worked in movies. My wife came and so did Michael Sheard and his wife. I didn't say that much but I learnt a lot.

CHAPTER 24

John Wroath

DURING MY TELEVISION chat show days I was twice bitterly disappointed when I had to let down one of my favourite Island musicians, the very charismatic John Wroath. I had interviewed him as my Sports Personality in the *Weekly Post*, when he'd helped to form our Wight Rhinos American Football team. When I did my *Hannam* TV12 chat shows he was included in my first batch of recorded programmes, made on April 4, 1998. The boss phoned to apologise to say six of the shows in the can had been lost. One of these featured John Wroath. Nine years later he recorded a Solent TV slot on *Hannam's Half Hour* and the station folded before it came to air. He took his disappointments so well.

It was not all bad news. He did appear on IW *Radio's John Hannam Meets* and at the second attempt finally made my TV12 show, in 2000.

Over the years I'd watched John in Sporting Life and the Wayward Sons. Both brilliant local bands. There have been quite a few connotations of Sporting Life, featuring, primarily, him and Duncan Jones.

John was mentioned in my last book, by the former Newport barber Jack Plucknett. He went into Jack's salon and asked for his head to be shaved and requested 15 tram lines on one side. The customer was always right, so Jack obliged. The next day he was visited by John's father, a local judge, who went in to complain

When John came on to my radio show The Wayward Sons had made both the national papers and TV. John was reported to have run off with his father's court wig to sing a song called *Just Like Murder*. Was it true? Or was it another made up story by a notorious local journalist? For once, John would give nothing away. He said: "I will give the same statement as my father has while all this has been going on. I am aware of the situation but at this stage do not want to make a comment. There's been a lot of publicity and the incident happened just before Cowes Week, when people were looking for a lot of silly stories. It was talked about at some cocktail party and the next thing I knew it was everywhere."

I loved to go and watch John perform. He has always been one of those rare breed of performers that you just can't take your eyes off. His bass playing has always been very visual and there is never a dull moment when he's on stage. John is another of our musicians who really should have made the big time. The Wayward sons made some superb records, including a fantastic six-song EP. They supported Jason Donovan at Ryde Arena. Sporting Life once took two 50 seater coaches to London to see the band perform at the Mean Fiddler.

Music has always been his life – alongside drinking Guinness and supporting Chelsea. He did head to London to pursue a dream but eventually came back to the Island and became a local professional musician.

The day John came live into my radio show we had a couple of phone calls from people complaining about him being on the show. That was even before he went on air. He was great entertainment.

I did have one very welcome tip off from a guy who revealed a John Wroath story. Later he didn't deny it on air – although he was a little horrified when I brought it up. Apparently on his 20th birthday he was debagged by some of his mates and was seen streaking though Newport. Unfortunately, his mother's best friend just happened to be driving by at the time.

CHAPTER 25

Pat Fergusson

I HAVE ALWAYS LOVED the prisoner of war escape movies like *Albert* RN, *The Great Escape* and, of course, *The Colditz Story*. In 1999 I was so thrilled to meet a former prisoner of Colditz, Major Pat Fergusson, who lived in Colwell Bay. Such was his popularity on *John Hannam Meets* he came twice within five weeks – after a little gentle persuasion from me.

Pat initially wanted to join the navy but failed because of his eyesight and so he chose the army. He did all his pre-war training and was commissioned in 1939. He joined the Royal Tank Regiment and eventually went to serve in France. It was there where he was first captured by the Germans. He'd been sent to reconnoitre a small French village. He parked his motor bike and after dark walked through the ravaged village looking to see if there were any other troops around and walked straight into the Germans.

During his wartime career he was sent to different prisoner of war camps because he had successfully escaped on several occasions. The first being when he jumped from the tailboard of a lorry and made a run for it. Within a few days he was caught. Two later attempts were very daring but he ended up being recaptured after well planned escapes.

Pat Fergusson with, above, Colditz Castle

In one camp he successfully got out via a tunnel they had dug from the cellar under their only brick block. This led under the wire to a new compound and brick building being built for Russian prisoners. The two of them were dressed as German workers and managed to get into this compound and then used ice skating boots, sent out by the Red Cross, to cut the outer wire being prepared for the new Russian prisoners.

"We had come up with a brilliant idea of how to get rid of the soil from our tunnel. We asked the Germans if we could have a long garden outside of the building. They were delighted and even gave us plants. Nobody noticed the garden had grown in height day by day. In the end it was a foot higher."

Once out, they headed for Switzerland but never made it.

On another dangerous attempt, from a different camp, Pat was one of the main diggers and they dug it under the wire and a road and up a hill to a chicken coop.

"Once I was so near to the road that I could see the grass roots, feel the wind and hear voices. I also was the only one to dig up the hill. That was tough. I was one of 30 who got out on the first night."

After being caught again he eventually ended up in Colditz. He was there when they built the famous glider which they planned to fly from the top of the castle. It was partly built by old floorboards donated by the Germans to enable them to build a table tennis table. They also used parts of their wooden beds.

"When we built the half-size test model and launched it into the courtyard the Germans were delighted and thought we were making boys toys and not planning escapes."

The eventual arrival of the Americans meant the glider was never flown.

I asked him what was his worst experience in the war – and had a shock.

"Flying back from Germany in a Dakota. The pilot was unhappy. He was short of fuel and at one stage asked us released prisoners of war to stand in the tail to get the trim right. We were also buzzed by two German fighters still around."

CHAPTER 26

David Icke

MUCH HAS BEEN written about David Icke since that amazing revelation on the Wogan television show. Some listened to him but many more quickly dismissed him as a crank. That 'Son of God' thing made him world famous and he's never stopped talking since. He sells out major venues all around the world and people from many countries seek his thoughts on current problems. In 2018 he was filming in London and taxi drivers stopped their cabs to talk to him. That was the last time I interviewed him. He might be

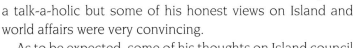

a talk-a-holic but some of his honest views on Island and world affairs were very convincing.

As to be expected, some of his thoughts on Island council officials and ferry companies had to be well censored before appearing in print. At least he wasn't live on air.

I first met David in 1985 and I took to him straight away. For many of us in the media he was a god of a different kind. A supreme television presenter right at the top of his game. The guys loved his knowledge and presentation of the sports he covered and to the ladies he was rather a hunky figure to admire while they were forced to watch sports they might not have liked.

At the time of our first meeting, thousands of pounds was being spent on commercial television to promote the Island. Ironically, on BBC television David Icke made a statement that money couldn't buy. His comment was: "I think the Isle of Wight is the greatest place on earth." That was not because he had recently moved here.

From the age of three he fell in love with steam trains and that passion is still with him. You can tell that when you sit in his Ryde flat. How did that all begin?

"When my dad could afford it we spent our annual holidays on the Island. For a mere 15 shillings you could enjoy a week of run-about excursions to Ventnor, Ryde, Newport, Freshwater and Cowes. I was gutted when they closed them all down."

The first time I interviewed David was actually in the workshop of the Havenstreet Steam Railway. He was in his element.

His life story has been well chronicled. He was all set to become a professional footballer but rheumatoid arthritis set in and he was forced to quit Coventry City. He did make a brief comeback and helped Hereford win promotion to the Third Division. They went on a Spanish tour to celebrate. On their return he had real problems.

"I went to bed one night as a footballer and woke up the next morning a cripple. Overnight, every bone in my body seized up and I couldn't walk for weeks. That was the end of my football career."

Later, after moving to the Island, he came to the aid of Ryde Sports when they were short of goalkeepers. That was his specialist position and he played a few games in the Island League.

After becoming a journalist on a small Leicester paper he joined Birmingham's top commercial station, BRMB Radio, and ended up a top TV presenter. Millions watched him on the televised snooker programmes. He also presented *Grandstand*, *The Nine O'Clock News* and was seen on *Saturday Superstore*.

David has lived here since the 80s and has been in the same Ryde flat for over 20 years. You might spot him in a local tea shop. He loves a cuppa and a natter.

Last year I wanted a picture of David and myself for *The Beacon* magazine. We were both hopeless at selfies so I nipped into the street and managed to persuade a lady to take our picture. She was thrilled to meet him and told him she'd been in the same pub quiz team as his son.

CHAPTER 27

Fiona Gwinnett

WHEN I WAS RUNNING the IW Amateur Theatre Awards for 17 years I often saw people I would love to interview but it was not really possible. I had no allegiance to any local company and did not want to be seen to favour any actors. I had enjoyed so many performances from Fiona Gwinnett and she had won several awards for top quality acting. I was also always fascinated by her changing array of hairstyles.

Fiona came to my home to pre-record her appearance on my chat show. Amazingly, it was the first time I had ever seen her away from a theatre. Before we got down to any serious chat I wanted to know about her bold choices of hairstyles. Apparently, it may well have been influenced by the fact that she once was a punk.

"I have never had my hair any longer than just grazing my shoulders. Now I let my hairdresser do as she pleases and I go along with it."

Being an Islander, Fiona began acting at the Young Vectis Players and has never looked backed. Initially, she wanted to be a nursery nurse and studied at the IW College. She was never happy and made a decision to leave in search of a new career – and that came with 22 years service in the RAF.

"I always remember taking the form home for my father to sign. He was a bit sniffy and called me a butterfly brain and when was I going to stick at anything at all." Sadly, he died in 1988 but after the first ten years she had the satisfaction of proving to him that she had settled down in a worthwhile job.

Fiona was one of only two ladies working in the intelligence department of the RAF and it was tough to contend with. They had a lot to put up with and were really intimidated. It was then a man's world.

"Some of it was in good humour but some was certainly not. Things that were said and done to us were not good."

For many years Fiona worked in Berlin and was on night duty when the Wall finally came down. When they went out, after their duty, there were sights and sounds that will live with her for ever.

"Ironically, when the Wall came down more doors closed for me and my career and it was Lincolnshire here I come."

While in Berlin she attended a meeting that would, in due course, change her life completely. It was a domestic abuse awareness day and that had such an affect on her. She found out many things that were difficult to accept.

Eventually after having had four children during her RAF career she made the tough decision to leave. It was not good for family life to be away from them for six months at a time, every couple of years or so.

"My first job on leaving the RAF was being part time at the Boston Women's Aid group, where I ran a centre."

That eventually led her back to her roots. Fiona was visiting her sister here on the Island and saw an advert in the *County Press* for a position at our Women's Refuge. She had already just taken another job and was happy. Despite feeling it would be wrong to leave her new job, she did ring on the last day that the applications were due to be in. Once they knew her qualifications they interviewed her straight away and gave her the job. When I interviewed her she was the chief executive of our Island refuge, which is open to both men and women.

Thankfully, she is still acting and proving an asset to any company she appears with. She does worry a little about being typecast in certain roles. Many of these can be quite noisy and confrontational. It's partly her fault, for being so good at them.

CHAPTER 28

Josh Barry

THE STORY OF Josh Barry is quite remarkable. He was born at St Mary's with Athetoid Cerebral Palsy and his parents were told he was going to die. A born fighter, young Josh survived and since then he's captured the hearts of so many people, including me.

In 2016, quite out of the blue, I had a message to go to Josh's home in East Cowes for a chat. He wanted to meet me, as he shared my love for the great old days of light entertainment. Being born in the town, I always love to go back and rekindle old memories of spending the first 32 years of my life there. I was also intrigued by Josh's request to meet me. It turned out that he was making an audio documentary called *Following The Money*, which was the story of the British theatrical agent, and he wanted to talk to me about some of the famous people I had interviewed over the past 44 years. I was delighted to be asked – although I had no idea what it would lead to. A lot of hard work? Don't mention it!

Josh has interviewed many people from the entertainment industry – with a difference. He is so knowledgeable about the halcyon days of British showbusiness and plots all his questions with great skill. Then one of his carers actually puts the questions to Jimmy Tarbuck, Barry Cryer, Nicholas Parsons, Brian Conley and numerous others.

During our first meeting he casually mentioned he would like me to host his special night at the Gurnard Pines Holiday Centre, where extracts of the documentary would be played and guests would be coming from the mainland. How could I refuse? He must have known I'm a soft touch.

Before the night, which proved a huge success, there was a trip to London to meet some of the key guests who were going to attend his event. I interviewed them to help plug the evening. These were people so well known within the business. Legends like Mike Dixon, Colin Edmunds and Dick Fiddy. I quickly realised how much genuine affection and admiration they had for Josh. Here was a young guy who was so interested in the contributions that had each made in their particular fields of entertainment. They all willingly had given up their time to support and encourage Josh – and they all travelled to Gurnard.

The Pines evening was one of the most enjoyable of my life. It was Josh's night and there was such a lot of real emotion. It had taken me hours to put it together but it was so worth it. There was a full house - and didn't he look smart.

When I interviewed him for *The Beacon* he was very honest and his great sense of humour came through. I have teased him on numerous occasions and he always comes back with a great response.

"Luckily for me, my Cerebral Palsy only affects me physically. The messages from my brain become mixed and consequently I suffer from unwanted movement. Yet, without wishing to use a cliché, I have never wanted my disability to define who I am."

Throughout his school and university days Josh has always had such a positive attitude. He had goals and has achieved many of them.

"I always knew that as a result of my difficulties with speech the chance of emulating my heroes was very slim. Instead, I have channelled my interests in the hope of working behind the scenes."

I was delighted to be asked to write the foreword to his wonderful book called *Adapted*.

I won't enlarge on the rumour that he was once seen sat in his wheelchair at a Cardiff strip club. Not Josh Barry, surely!!

CHAPTER 29

Joan Yule

THE FIRST TIME I ever saw Joan Yule was back in the early 50s. As a young schoolboy, I was so thrilled when my grandfather took me to watch East Cowes Vics play football at Whippingham. I had an instant hero. It was their goalkeeper Scotty Yule and I can still vividly remember his yellow jersey and the fact he often ran out to the halfway line.

Among the wives of the players was Joan Yule. They certainly weren't called wags in those days – but they were regulars in the stand and continually gave vocal encouragement. They were happy and couldn't care less about the latest fashions.

I really got to know Joan well at the Towers Holiday Camp, at Thorness Bay. Her old boss, Fred Sage, is featured in a previous chapter of this book. It was classic H*i-de-Hi!*, as you will have found out in Fred's chapter.

I can remember when Joan rang me to say that one of Europe's greatest footballers, Southampton's Ron Davies, was making an appearance at The Towers. He was also a gifted artist and was marketing some of his work.

Joan began her life as a DJ at The Towers. They had their resident three piece band and their drummer was Don White. His son, Snowy, who first began playing music at the camp, went on to enjoy numerous hit records including the haunting B*ird Of Paradise*. Joan, who could put her hand to anything, willingly agreed to put on a few records in the band's break. It was purely the greats of the era, like Nat King Cole, Ella Fitzgerald and Frank Sinatra. When the Beatles came along she borrowed her daughter's records to keep the youngsters happy. When I last interviewed Joan she was 91 years old – and still listening to music.

When one of the national companies took over The Towers, Joan moved on and ended up on Shanklin Pier. Due to her age she was affectionately known as the DJ gran. On a visit to the town's Acorn Records store, to add to her collection of vinyl, she asked for the receipt to be made out to Shanklin Pier. The young assistant said: "They tell me an old gal plays all the records down there." Joan never said a word.

The bikers, mods and head bangers who frequented the pier loved our Joan. She could quickly suss out her audience and suddenly Status Quo, T Rex and the Small Faces could be heard halfway across the bay.

In 1987 her sad story went all around the world. Shanklin Pier was blown away in the hurricane and her 2000 records sank to the bottom of the sea.

"We had a diver go down but he only found one record. I also lost my deck, speakers and lighting equipment. Albert the pier ghost got all those records that had taken me 30 years to collect. He must have had some rave-up," said Joan.

It would have taken more than a hurricane to end her DJ career. Later she surfaced at the Sandown Bay Holiday Centre. After her loss, I mentioned the fact she was looking for records in my *Weekly Post* column. True to form, Islanders came to her rescue and she even got back her favourite – Acker Bilk's *Stranger On The Shore*.

Once in a while Joan used to phone me up for a chat. That was always a pleasure and, of course, she was never lost for words.

I felt both sad and honoured when she rang and asked if I would do the eulogy at Scotty's funeral. It was such a privilege to pay tribute to my first local soccer hero.

CHAPTER 30

Jamie Lawrence

SUNDAY DECEMBER 20, 1992, is a Sunday lunchtime I will never forget. My listening figures went up, due to my one-off captive audience. The extra listeners were all about a mile from our studio. They were all inmates of the nearby Camp Hill Prison and one of their fellow prisoners, Jamie Lawrence, was released for an hour to appear live on my show. Camp Hill deputy governor, Eddie Walder, was more than happy to bring him in. Eddie, with the help of other members of staff and local football club manager Dale Young, had teamed up to change Jamie's life for ever.

As a youngster he was mad on football but eventually was led into a life that he later regretted. It had led him directly to Camp Hill. There he became an instant prison hero because of his amazing football talents. One or two local Island clubs took teams into the prison to play. They all came out raving about Jamie's soccer skills. Cowes Sports were one of them.

Dale Young had asked the prison authorities if Jamie could be released every other Saturday to play in Cowes Sports home games in the Wessex League. They finally agreed, as a part of a Camp Hill 21 project, and this trial period worked out brilliantly for both Jamie and Cowes Sports. This instant success meant he was allowed to play in away games as well.

"At the end of a game I was given a Guinness, my favourite drink, before being driven back to the prison. Dale used to give me five packets of mints so it wasn't discovered."

Jamie's emergence as a Wessex League footballer drew scouts from many clubs. Portsmouth were interested and Southampton watched him five times. He made both national and local newspaper headlines.

On my show, he promised to go straight and told me: "Being sent to Camp Hill was the best thing that could have happened to. I just want to become a professional footballer." I gave him a present of a football book, which included details of clubs and their grounds.

Jamie was released on July 13, 1993. He did achieve his dream. Within a few months he joined Sunderland. At Camp Hill he'd earned £5 a week. At Roker Park he was given a £10,000 signing on fee and £300 a week. He went on to play in the Premiership for both Bradford and Leicester City, where his wages went up considerably. He also played

for Doncaster Rovers, Walsall, Wigan, Grimsby and Brentford.

In the Premiership with Leicester he won a Coca Cola Cup Final winners medal. He was also capped 24 times by Jamaica, the birthplace of his father. When Mexico played Jamaica there was a crowd of 105,000.

Jamie made many national publications and was the first professional footballer to display the pineapple haircut. On *Match Of The Day* you could also pick him out by his coloured hair.

He also wrote his autobiography, *From Prison To The Premiership*, which was definitely not Mills and Boon material. He also became famous for his parties and spending. Wisely, he did also invest in property.

After his retirement, Jamie played, coached and managed in non-league football. I went to visit him a few years ago, when he was a fitness coach in London. I took Heather with me and it was a pleasure to meet him and be in his company. Later he returned to the Island in his role as an official inspirational prison speaker.

I was certainly very moved in 2006 when he sent me a personal text following the sad news of Heather's death. I will never forget his kind thought.

CHAPTER 31

Phil Hancock

ONCE WHEN my heating engineer, Neil Gurney, came for my annual service he invited me to talk to Ryde Rotary Club, for a second time. He told me he was going to sit me next to a guy who had an amazing story. That's all he would tell me. How right he was. Phil Hancock's story included the Beatles, Cliff Richard, Kate Bush, ELO, Pink Floyd and André Previn. He'd worked at Abbey Road, the world's most famous recording studio, for 32 years.

Phil left school and was advised to take up an apprenticeship. He tried BP, the GPO and EMI. The latter offered him the chance of a career.

"I was sent to an EMI factory in Feltham where they did work for the Ministry of Defence. It involved sea to air missiles. After nearly five years I got bored and asked for a transfer to their music department, which didn't go down too well. I got sent to the record factory at Hayes then eventually changed departments and started to make equipment for Abbey Road studios. I was sent there to install it and decided that was the place I wanted to be."

It was white coat and collar and tie job and when George Martin left to go to Air, his own studio, he took some engineers with him. Phil took one of the vacancies at Abbey Road. Being young and working at a job he loved was just perfect for him. He also volunteered for extra studio work at evenings and weekends as the older guys did not want it.

Phil worked on some epic recordings. These included Pink Floyd's *Dark Side Of The Moon*, *I'm Nearly Famous*, the album that revitalised Cliff Richard's career, Wings classic *Band On The Run* and Kate Bush's *The Man With The Child In His Eyes*. He was in his element.

Paul McCartney realised Phil's engineering skills and always wanted him on his sessions. When McCartney had a studio build under his offices, Phil did some work for him.

"I really liked Paul and his wife Linda was such a lovely lady. Sometimes when Wings were recording if it got too noisy in the studio I used to babysit their son, James, in a quieter room.

"They had a donkey called Jet and once brought him into the studio. I don't know which came first, Jet the donkey or their hit song."

Phil worked with all the Beatles. He engineered on George Harrison's album called *All Things Must Pass*, which was produced by Phil Spector. Ringo Starr also played on that album. Also he worked on records by John Lennon and Yoko.

Phil, who got several promotions, also worked on outside location recordings. These included the top selling Max Boyce live albums, Reginald Dixon's last ever album at the Tower Ballroom, Blackpool and the Wurzels live in Somerset.

One lunchtime when he was working at Paul McCartney's London studio he got an urgent message to go to the Studio Pathe Marconi in Paris, as they had a technical problem with a Cliff Richard recording session. Phil got there by the evening and managed to sort the problem straight away. He had worked on numerous records by Cliff and The Shadows.

Phil will never forget the night he was taken out to dinner by André Previn and his wife Mia Farrow. He had so much respect for André.

In 32 years at Abbey Road he worked with such diverse characters as Mrs Mills, Jeff Lynne, Geoff Love, Roy Wood and Eric Clapton.

"Music breaks down all barriers. I was lucky to be in the right place at the right time."

CHAPTER 32

Jack Whitehead

AN ACCIDENT at a wartime RAF aerodrome in Gloucestershire was the reason Jack Whitehead became one of the most respected worldwide figurehead carvers. It changed his life completely and sent his career into a new and exciting adventure, which was never planned. He was injured trying to start an Auster engine. The propeller backfired, with his hand still on it. During his recovery period he needed something to try to get his hands working again. He told the doctors he liked doing a little woodcarving and, with their consent, he tried it again and they improved quite quickly. Ironically, it was a fortunate accident.

Initially, after the war Jack worked as a sculptor for a touring puppet company. Eventually he was employed by the famous Lanchester's puppet family, which led him

to television's *Muffin The Mule* series, with Annette Mills. On one occasion Jack was involved with a show for Winston Churchill and his family at Chequers.

"George Bernard Shaw had written a special play for puppets and we performed it on a Boxing Day. Winston wanted to know how they worked and tried them himself. He also compared some of the characters to his Labour opposition," said Jack.

Because he was good at hanging things on strings, Jack was offered a job on the hit television series called *The Invisible Man*. They made 52 x 30-minute shows in a year. The series won so much acclaim for its amazing special effects. He was the brains behind many of these, which included the impressions in the chairs, as the invisible man sat down, and his lighted cigarette which seemed to virtually float across the screen. You never saw the star of the show – other than the occasional glimpse of a bandage around a face.

Jack was also involved in a near fatality in Shalfleet Creek. They were making a movie for the Children's Film Foundation and one of the stars was a nine year cockney kid called Dennis Waterman. He had to jump in but couldn't swim and it took several takes, as Dennis was frightened. On his fourth attempt he made it but disappeared from view. Jack was driving the cabin cruiser but couldn't see him. Suddenly, much to everyone's delight, he surfaced near the stern in his yellow lifejacket, having gone right under the boat. The panic was over. Dennis once confirmed this story on a *Wogan* TV show.

When Jack was asked by a guy from Wootton Creek, where he also lived on a houseboat for 18 years, to carve a figurehead of a mermaid to go with them to New Zealand, it led to an amazing career. With young local lad Norman Gaches as his assistant, they became very much in demand. Jack did seven London Boat Shows and others in Toronto, New York and Miami. He also spent three years in Honolulu.

Jack's most famous being the 15 foot figurehead for *The Warrior*. Locally famous were his horse on top of the Ponda Rosa roadhouse and the totem pole at the Little Canada Holiday Centre.

An American tourist was passing the Ponda Rosa and saw Jack holding up his horse, ready to go on the roof. Apparently, he marvelled at Jack's immense strength. I hope someone told him it wasn't real.

"When I look back, my career was never planned at all. It was something I wanted to do and it just turned out that way."

Jack's two sons are also in this book. There is a chapter on Mike and his other son, Robbie, is pictured in our old Five Alive pop band.

CHAPTER 33

Pat Reader

WHEN I WAS AT Cowes Secondary Modern there was a buzz of anticipation when we were told a girl from a convent school was going to join us. What was she going to be like? Different to what we'd imagined, that's for sure. Pat Reader was such fun and most of us boys fell in love with her – including me. I think I called her my girlfriend for a week or two. I remember she knew more about life than we did. It was still a surprise, a year or so later, when she became a pop star.

Although I lived about 100 yards from the East Cowes Town Hall, I never saw her in her previous school's production of the light operetta *Blue Eyed Susan*. Apparently, she was a hit and had stolen the show.

Her late father, Reg, had been the instigator of her pop music career and she did win an Island cinema talent contest. That led her to London singing lessons with Maurice Burman, which were not a success. Apparently he tried to get all his pupils to sing like Ella Fitzgerald. She did so much better with Mabel Corran. Her pupils had included Dickie Valentine, Marion Ryan, Mark Wynter and Craig Douglas.

Young Pat was then sent to gain experience in northern clubs. That was tough for a 16-year old from the Island. She sometimes followed the stripper and the intoxicated customers often wanted more than a few pop songs. Things did get better and she worked in theatre shows and tours with David Hughes, Bob Monkhouse, Jill Day, Smokey Robinson and Ricky Valance. She also made cabaret appearances at top London venues, including the Colony Club and the Stork Room.

Pat also made records and in 1960 made her debut on Triumph Records, whose other artists included Michael Cox and George Chakiris. The songs were *Ricky*, written by her pianist Vic Smith, and *Dear Daddy*, a Joe Henderson song. The Johnny Keating Orchestra backed her.

Her second single, *Cha Cha On The Moon*, was her most successful and has been released on several compilation CDs in recent years. It was produced by the legendary Joe Meek and recorded at his famous Holloway Road studio. There was a brilliant movie made about his career called *Telstar*. *Cha Cha* was actually used later on the soundtrack of the 1999 movie *The Bachelor*. In all, Pat released four singles.

During our first-ever interview, back in 1977, Pat told me her true feelings about that period of he life.

"I was just basically lazy and really didn't put too much into it. If I had got my big break it might have encouraged me a little more. I suppose I didn't have the right attitude."

Pat came back to the Island and has never moved away again. For a while she ran a Cowes pub with her husband, which was where I first interviewed her. They were, subsequently, divorced and she became a nurse at St Mary's for many years. She remarried but her husband died a year or two ago.

Pat got tempted back into singing by her daughter Traci. It all began with Pat singing *Who's Sorry Now* in an original Island musical called *My Girl*, at Ventnor Winter Gardens. That led to a few other local appearances with Craig Douglas, Marty Wilde and Alvin Stardust, at the Medina Theatre, Newport. She was also featured on Craig's highly acclaimed 2011 album, *The Craig Douglas Project*, which was produced by Andy Gray.

Edward Griffiths, Pat's grandson, is now a professional singer and so popular on cruise ships. He travels the world and has a greater love for the business than his grandmother ever had. Reg Reader would be so proud.

CHAPTER 34

Gareth Williams

IN 1983 THE ISLAND'S Gareth Williams, then a rather naive teenager, went to Southend Football Club to start a career as an apprentice professional footballer. With their manager being the legendary Bobby Moore, it must have seemed rather daunting to a shy kid from the Isle of Wight. He became homesick and left after two weeks. There was a happy ending and during his second chance career he played in the Premiership for Aston Villa and in total made around 300 appearances for several other Football League clubs.

I followed Gareth's career very closely and interviewed him on several occasions. I noticed how his confidence grew as he matured as both a person and footballer. Watching him play for Villa was an exciting experience. Suddenly our Gareth was playing against Arsenal, Chelsea, Manchester United and Liverpool. If he hadn't left Island League side Whitecroft Barton to sign for East Cowes Vics, it might never have happened.

Gareth has always paid his respects to local soccer personalities who worked on his early potential. Names like Guiseppe Cretella, Peter Holmes, Peter Groves and Keith Amey all helped to broaden his football skills.

"I also remember those three great seasons under Jock Horne at Whitecroft Barton. Jock was such a great motivator. When I needed a kick up the backside, he was the one who gave it to me. It was Jock who always put me straight when I fell out of line," said Gareth, back in 1993.

When he signed for Graham Daish at East Cowes Vics it proved the turning point, as his talents were noted along the south coast.

"At the Vics we never lost for over 70 games and must have had the best all-Island forward line ever. It was great to play alongside Mark Deacon and Steve Greening. They were great players and unlucky not to make professional football."

To pursue his dream of making professional football, the second time around, he signed for Gosport Borough, then a Southern League side. His skills were seen further afield and talents scouts from Liverpool, Leicester City and Aston Villa were hot on his trail. Hence his dream move to Villa Park.

Amazingly, he'd previously scored in trials at both Pompey and Saints, and played well, but neither club was prepared to sign him. Long before that, he'd played one game for Newport and scored two goals – then didn't turn up for training.

"They never made contact anymore. In your teens you do things like that but I've grown up now."

At Aston Villa, for manager Graham Taylor, Gareth made his debut at Crystal Palace. There was also a festive season he'll never forget.

"We were training on Christmas night when Chris Price pulled a muscle. Graham told me I was in, if Chris was unfit. At 11am on Boxing Day, 1989, I was told I was in against Manchester United, at noon. There was 42,000 in the ground and I barely had time to get nervous." Incidentally, Villa won 3-0 and Gareth was man of the match.

Despite being a striker, Villa played him as a full back. This surprised many of his Island fans.

During his long career Gareth went on to play for Barnsley, Hull, Northampton and Scarborough. During this period he scored 48 goals. Later he moved into coaching and managed Matlock Town.

When he played for Barnsley against Southend, he scored a hat trick. I wonder if anyone from the Roots Hall club remembered their old two week apprentice.

CHAPTER 35

Kenny Mac & Les Maskell

IN 1988 I MANAGED to complete an East Cowes family double, in my two columns in the *Weekly Post*. Ken Maskell, who was on my *Stage Talk* page, was the easiest to achieve – he lived less than a mile from where I was born and I knew him as bandleader Kenny Mac. His brother, Les, my Sports Personality, was harder to track down. He lived in

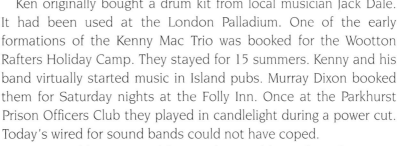

Diss, Norfolk. There had always been rumours in the town about this local footballer who played for Norwich City.

When I interviewed Ken Maskell, (alias Kenny Mac), he was still fronting his own band at the age of 67. Every Friday night they had at least 100 regular fans who attended their dinner dances at the Melville Hall, Sandown. What a bargain at just £5 a head. Those were the days. Now it would cost you more just to park in the town for a few hours.

Ken originally bought a drum kit from local musician Jack Dale. It had been used at the London Palladium. One of the early formations of the Kenny Mac Trio was booked for the Wootton Rafters Holiday Camp. They stayed for 15 summers. Kenny and his band virtually started music in Island pubs. Murray Dixon booked them for Saturday nights at the Folly Inn. Once at the Parkhurst Prison Officers Club they played in candlelight during a power cut. Today's wired for sound bands could not have coped.

Kenny Mac

Once Ken took a nine year old music-mad boy and two of his pals to his gig at Wootton Rafters. The youngster was keen to become a drummer and Ken gave him his first lesson. He never made the big time as a drummer but has become one of the most influential bass players in the world. It was our own Mark King.

What of Ken's brother Les? Yes he had played for Norwich City and scored 224 goals for the Canaries. So my mother was right about the local boy made good.

Les had played for the all-conquering East Cowes Grange Road school team. Two of their teachers, 'Butterfly' Moth and 'Nanner' Weeks, put the fear into all their pupils.

"One of my greatest early memories was skippering the Island Boys team who beat Southampton in the Hampshire Shield final, at Dean Park, Bournemouth. I was centre half and the guy I marked, Norman Cantlin, went on to play for England," said Les.

When he joined Norwich he got £3 a week. When he was in the first team it rose to £7. No expensive wags around in those days! For a former defender he could find the net. For Norwich he got six in one game, five on four separate occasions, hit a four and also four hat tricks. One of his team mates at Carrow Road was Ted Bates, who later did wonders as the manager of Southampton.

In reality, the war interfered with the careers of so many top footballers, including Les. He did play in the Wartime League for Norwich, Northampton, Aldershot and Ipswich. When he played for Aldershot he was the only non-international in the team.

Les Maskell's professional career lasted from 1936 to 1948. Then, thinking of his future, he declined a move to Northampton and went into non-league football. That also gave him the chance to run The Greyhound Inn, in Diss, for 32 years. It was what old footballers did in those days.

The Maskell boys did us proud.

Les Maskell

CHAPTER 36

Joan Sherry

I MET THE delightfully eccentric Joan Sherry back in 1977, when I went to Morton Common to interview her husband Peter. He was one of the famous Five Sherry Brothers, who sang, danced, played instruments and provided comedy. He told me he had plans to write a book but, sadly, he died before this materialised. Four years later I went back to the Devonia Caravan Park to talk to Joan about her brand new book. She had fulfilled his dream.

Joan, who was known professionally as Linda Hagan, had quite a career herself. In her early days she was a mezzo-soprano and during the war she worked for Bill Scott-Gordon, who later produced summer season shows at Sandown Pavilion. For a while she became one of the Southern Sisters, who were resident singers with Henry Hall.

Then, with her enormous vocal range and a real flair for comedy, she began to appear in top seaside resident shows. These included Llandudno and Blackpool. She also worked with the National Light Opera Company.

In 1955 she spent the summer on Sandown Pier with two very funny comedians, Felix Bowness and Leslie Adams. This was for Bill Scott-Gordon's Revels company. Bill had tempted her back to showbusiness, after she had retired due to her husband's poor health. Joan and Peter spent that summer here in their caravan and came back a year later to buy Devonia.

For some years Joan, as Linda Hagan, became one of the Island's most sought after cabaret artists.

"At one time there was only Harry Dawson and me doing that sort of thing. We were part of the furniture," said Joan.

Joan's repertoire contained such a wide variety of songs from *The Biggest Aspidistra In The World* to *Summertime*. Her book, *Dance For Your Uncle Sam*, was actually inspired by a much more contemporary song, David Gates classic number one ballad *If*, a hit for his own group, Bread, and Telly Savalas. In her latter years Joan wrote her own songs for the first time.

In the early 70s she starred with Cyril Amey in *Hello Dolly* for the Sandown Amateur Operatic Society. They would completely sell out the venue every Easter.

Joan was up for anything – and would burst into song wherever she was. Her beautiful voice just stunned people. At the age of 80, she flew to America to sing in San Francisco's Episcopal Cathedral in front of 1800 people, with no nerves at all. She was virtually mobbed at the end. They loved one of her own songs. Then she flew to San Antonio, in Texas, to sing her songs to both Americans and Mexicans.

"The Mexicans cried buckets at my songs. They had come over the border to escape a terribly brutal life and poor conditions. My songs were about people who had suffered and they knew all about that."

"I also met up with two missionaries, Hector and Maria Malav, who had spent several years at our Verbum Dei Centre."

We were often invited by Joan to that Carisbrooke centre where she did so much to help. She was a perfect host and seemed to have a flock of admirers.

Joan always made such a fuss of me and she invited Heather and I to dinner at Morton Common. It was a night to remember – in more ways than one. She served us a chicken meal and we both brought it back up in the early hours of the following morning. We were quite ill – and I never had the courage to ring Joan to see if she had the same problem. We were invited back several times but, conveniently, we always had something on. Well – we told her we did!

CHAPTER 37

Edward 'Ted' Satherley

TED SATHERLEY was the Island's mobile librarian for over 30 years and during that spell he drove 500,000 miles around our roads and issued six million books. He worked on his own and had stops from five minutes to two hours.

When Ted first joined the Island's library service, the Newport branch had a closed access. Potential readers were not allowed into the rooms of books. The assistants had to ask what books they were interested in and would bring up to a dozen for them to choose from. They were long hours. Ted worked from 9.30 until lunch at 1pm, then from 2.30 to 5pm and then after a tea break from 6-8pm. All for £34 a year.

There were so many stories he could relate.

"One day I was parked at a farm place and the family were out and there was a girl there I knew who was about 18. I was about 20 and not married. I tooted my van horn and she popped her head out of an upstairs window and said she was in the bath and would not be long. I told her I was in a hurry and could she come as she was. After about two minutes this large white bath towel came into the van. I said you're not – and she said 'I am' – and she was!"

Once when he was parked outside of Chale Stores, opposite the allotments, the local policeman came into the van dressed in his gardening clothes to choose his books. Apparently, he looked like Worzel Gummidge. A family on holiday pulled up behind the van and the husband looked in the back of the van and said: "You people over here can read then." Quick as a flash, PC Gurd replied "I'll be down in a minute to read your licence and check your tyres."

Ted found many items left in books. These included £20, a pair of scissors, a slice of streaky bacon, a marriage licence for later that day and a condom. He was relieved to find the last object was still in the packet.

When he visited Parkhurst Prison he was usually asked for murder mysteries or crime thrillers. He had to turn down a request for a book on lock and key making.

Ted could never forget a posh new riding mac he bought in RC Gray's in Newport.

"I was courting my lovely wife Betty and we went for a walk over Mount Joy on a very dark night and I was wearing my expensive new cream coat. We got to the top and, rather craftily, I told her I was tired and could we lie down for a while. We got into the field and I laid down my new coat. We got down on it and after a couple of minutes Betty, who was wearing new American open top shoes, said she could feel something hot and sticky between her toes. We quickly got up and right in the middle of my coat was a huge cow pat. I managed to get it in past my mother. I put it in the bath and trampled on it like grapes. I got it out but it was never quite the same."

Once, on leave from the army, he caught a late night ferry to Ryde, during the blackout. It was so dark and he went into the ladies toilets by mistake and had to hide in a cubicle for the whole journey.

During his life Ted had to recover from several family tragedies. His son was born with no arms, in the thalidomide era, and his daughter died so young. I admired him so much for the way he recovered to enjoy life and his beloved cricket.

CHAPTER 38

Jeff Manners

JEFF MANNERS was a very controversial Medina Borough councillor and he'd always resisted my requests for him to appear on my radio show. I finally persuaded him and it was a Sunday lunchtime to remember. Firstly, he was the first ever guest to cycle to the station. He even walked into the live studio with his cycle clips still on. He had a car at the time but was not allowed to drive it, for a reason he deeply regretted. As expected, he spoke his mind and the phone lines were red hot – and much to his surprise – they were all complimentary.

Jeff, centre, with Little & Large

There were the expected derogatory remarks about Maggie Thatcher, certain Island councillors and, of course, high praise for Manchester City, who then had an all-British team, and the rock group Queen. He was a great fan of Freddie Mercury.

Jeff started his working life as an apprentice for Blakes's the Newport printers. Later he worked for many years at the *County Press*. At one time he also ran his own security business.

Many remember him as a top local football referee who became a class one official in less than four years. On one occasion he abandoned a Sunday League game at Whitecroft because of the attitudes of most of the players in a very competitive match. He was impressed with the late Arnold Olive, who later apologised for the behaviour of the players. Arnie also went to the subsequent enquiry to confirm his post-match statement.

"I remember refereeing Brading in a Hampshire League game when Ginger Squibb was their manager. I overheard his pre-match team talk. He said to his team 'you know who the referee is today – it's that b-----d Manners. Just keep your mouth shut and get on with the game.' To me that summed up that they recognised my potential."

Jeff made local paper headlines when he decided to give up refereeing and had thrown all his medals and plaques into the dustbin. How did that come about?

"I'd had a short spell in hospital and was away from refereeing for some time. I didn't miss it or all the abuse I got at weekends. So I called it a day. I looked at the trophies and thought they were not a fair indication of my ability. I'd always thought that referees on the Island, because of our geographical position, never had a fair crack of the whip. Guys like Andy King and Graham Fowler should have made the Football League."

Jeff entered politics in 1978/79. "I was so incensed when the IW County Council made a 37.5% rate rise that I decided to put my name forward. Steve Ross, who was a real MP for the people of the Island, persuaded me to join the Liberal party. I then decided I was not going to be a political lackey for anyone." Many of us admired him for this.

"At early Medina Borough meetings I sat next to Roger Mazillius and I learnt such a lot from him, although he was a Tory. Actually, I think if the Conservatives had adopted him as their parliamentary candidate, I believe he might have just done it."

Once he made the huge front page banner headlines in the *Weekly Post*. When there was talk of the deployment of missiles in this country, he confessed he'd be happy to have a missile site in his own front garden, as long as it pointed East.

CHAPTER 39

Hilary Hall

I FIRST MET HILARY HALL in 1983, after seeing her HDH Dancers save a professional pantomime from a complete disaster, at Newport's Medina Theatre. My review of how a young Island troupe had saved the show sent me in search of this talented lady and she revealed the full story.

Apparently, they were not booked until late November and only met the professional cast at noon on the day it opened. They were still rehearsing at 6.30 and the show opened an hour later. Amazingly, a few years down the line I met one of the unknown young professionals in the cast. By then he was the really famous comedian and game show host Andrew O'Connor. Had I misjudged the show? Not really. He agreed the pantomime was rubbish but remembered the local dancers who stole the show.

I would have seen Hilary perform a few years before that show. She came to Warner's St Clare as a greencoat, with the intention of moving on from a principal dancer to perfect a cabaret act. At their first viewing her parents were not impressed with the complex. They even offered her a lift back home. It was tempting but she decided to stay and pursue her dream. Thankfully, thousands of Island youngsters benefitted from that decision.

Hilary grew up in Wiltshire and had been a member of the Tanwood Dancers, a professional group who performed in pantomimes and on TV's *Opportunity Knocks*. She also had her own Saturday dance school, which led to a full week's work and 300 pupils.

Hilary stayed on at St Clare and instead of commuting back to Wiltshire began freelance teaching here for the Elmwood and Susan Alexander dance schools. In 1980 she decided to open her own schools in Seaview and Wootton. Then she moved to Ryde and continued until she retired in 2013.

Over the years Hilary was able to enhance the dreams of many young Island dancers. Several of her former pupils have graced the West End and other major stages all around the world. These have included Traci Porter, Clare Bonsu, Gary Wood, Eloise Shutler and Hilary's own daughter Charlotte. The list is endless, as many have worked on cruise ships.

"Over the years I was so excited by seeing the potential in some of the youngsters who came to my Ryde school but it was not always about making young stars. That's a hard business to succeed in. My pupils always had fun as well. They were helped by the disciplines and the experiences they gained from appearing in shows," said Hilary.

I admired so many of her young dancers, particularly in her well constructed Medina Theatre showcases. Some had no real chance of making the big time but on stage they came alive and clearly enjoyed every minute. Others were so brave to even attempt dancing but the motivation changed their lives.

Hilary readily admitted, during our last interview in 2013, that her family life did suffer at times because of the demands of running such a thriving dance school. The lessons may have only been from 3 to 9pm but there was so much administration to handle, music to prepare, shows to organise and mainland visits, as an examiner.

The reception she received at the end of her last show, *Simply The Best*, proved what a huge impact she had made in those 33 years. On that occasion there was no hint of her pantomime principal boy role. Us dads loved her wonderful legs and teasing thigh slaps! Oh yes we did!

CHAPTER 40

Lawrence Holofcener

THE LAST TIME I met Julia Holofcener was in late 2018 at the reception before the first-ever reading of her late husband's play called *The Big Sleepover At The White House*, at London's Jermyn Street Theatre. I gave her a copy of my last book and told her that Larry was in the next one. "Whatever for?" was her instant reply. Julia is a great tease. Larry had written world famous songs like *Too Close For Comfort* and *Mr Wonderful*, danced in a Broadway show with Ginger Rogers, deputised for Anthony Newley in *Stop The World I Want To Get Off* and had sculptured the amazing London statue of Churchill and Roosevelt, where millions have joined them to sit on the seat in New Bond Street. Oh! – and I nearly forgot. He made his solo cabaret debut in Ventnor.

Larry Holofcener was an interviewers dream. He was modest but had an amazing all round talent and a fund of fascinating stories. He was a songwriter, playwright, author, sculptor, actor and painter. He also, as he proved in his solo cabaret debut at Ventnor's Royal Hotel, could interpret the lyric of a famous song in his own unique style.

His songs had been recorded by Sinatra, Sammy Davis, Ella Fitzgerald, Peggy Lee, Johnny Mathis and Michael Buble, to name but a few.

"It's a great thrill for any songwriter to have a song recorded. That's the ultimate, to simply get it recorded. You never know what's going to happen to it."

During our first interview at IW *Radio* it seemed almost unreal that Larry was singing along with his own lyric to Frank Sinatra's version of *Too Close For Comfort*. I did manage to surprise him late in the show by playing Ruby Murray's version of *Mr Wonderful*, which he had never heard.

It was not always so easy. In the early days of their song writing partnership Larry and Jerry Bock collaborated on over 50 songs that never even got recorded. Things did get a lot better and their musical called *Mr Wonderful* brought Sammy Davis to a new audience.

In his early days Larry actually worked for Radio WISD in Baltimore, his birthplace. He was so lucky to interview stars who were visiting the city. These included Nat King Cole and Frankie Laine.

While he was writing songs for the *Merv Griffin Show* he was offered the chance to escort some huge megastars to local theatres.

"There was I, a young guy, taking stars like Joan Crawford and Marlene Dietrich on my arm to theatres and restaurants. I just couldn't believe it," said Larry. I think they were called 'arm candy' for the stars.

In the early 60s Larry was amazed to deputise for Anthony Newley on Broadway, in *Stop The World I Want To Get Off*. He went on a few times and on one special Saturday he did both performances, as Newley was marrying Joan Collins. He had to do 16 songs in the show and dance. He surprised himself and pulled it off.

Larry appeared in the original Broadway production of *Hello Dolly* and danced with Carol Channing. When she left to head for the West End production, Ginger Rogers took over – and Larry danced with her every night.

In 2017 Julia presented Newport's Apollo Theatre with Larry's sculpture of Faces Of Olivier. Over 25 years Larry and Julia were regular visitors to the Island and lived in St Lawrence and Bembridge.

CHAPTER 41

Henry Barney

BACK IN 1970 Newport's Henry Barney won the most coveted trophy in world darts – the legendary *News of the World* Championship. He went from The Pointers Inn, Newchurch, to London's Alexandra Palace and cleaned up from an original entry of 150,000. It was just as well he won his first round tournament to become champion of his local Island pub.

It was long before the Keegan Brown era. There was no prize money in the kitty. All he won was a record player and he brought the cup back on the train to the Island. To reach the London final our Henry won the Island, Hampshire and London and Home Counties titles. When he won the Hampshire title he fell off the stage into the orchestra pit. He couldn't name that tune but he quickly got back on song to win through.

I loved interviewing the most famous darts player in the world, the late Eric Bristow. He was a great self-promoter and on several occasions was the best in the world. He told me during one of our interviews: "The *News of the World* title was reckoned to be the hardest trophy to win in the world. It was played from 501 and there were only three legs. If you lost the first you were in trouble."

Back to April 25, 1970, Henry had no real nerves on the day and as he came out of the Alexandra Palace, he looked up and saw his name in lights as the *News of the World* champion. He'd just been given the trophy by the wonderful Henry Cooper.

A few years earlier a workmate of mine at Gould, Hibberd and Randall's, Harry Woodford, from Newport's Malt and Hops pub, also got to a *News of the World* final. Harry just froze on stage in front of thousands of people. He could have beaten any of them back in the Malt and Hops.

Henry was actually offered £36 a week to be at the beck and call of the darts manufacturers for personal appearances all over Great Britain and beyond.

During our last interview, back in 2015, Henry told me the story.

"My wife had just had our son and I decided I just couldn't leave the family. I couldn't get sponsors on the Island and I even lost my job with Cheek Brothers. I visited a darts factory with the cup and had to have a day or so off – and was sacked because of it."

These days darts players practice for hours. Was that the case when Henry was the best in the land? "I didn't practice much at all. I was picking spuds and sprouts on farms and didn't have a lot of time."

When I last visited Henry I noticed a dartboard hung in the kitchen. I decided not to issue a challenge to either him or his daughter, April, who was also a rather good player. I'd only ever played once before, anyway.

Henry, who sadly died in 2018, played with 15 gram brass darts. He was lucky enough to play during the golden years of Island darts. In the 70s and 80s there were so many local leagues and we had so many brilliant players to give Henry a run for his money.

He actually retired from competitive darts when he was in his mid 70s. His last team came from the Ambassadors Club, in Gunville.

Henry was thrilled by the success of our Keegan Brown and was keen to praise him. "I wish young Keegan a great future. If he keeps his cool he needn't work for the rest of his life – just play darts."

CHAPTER 42

Ian Dockray

I WAS USED TO SEEING Ian Dockray in the Shorwell village pantomimes and loved it when he forgot his lines and made it up as he went along. You never quite knew what to expect. When I finally met him, off stage, he was younger and more handsome than I imagined. Mind you, he still looked too old to play Buttons in *Cinderella*, as he had done a few years earlier. On that occasion the remarks from his mates in the audience made it even more enjoyable. Cinders was probably too young to appreciate them.

Ian is such a likeable man and his life has been so eventful – and has included boxing, shoes, fish and chips, ironing, speed dating, karaoke, nightclubs and Hurricane Higgins.

In 2018, I was flattered to be invited to his Golden Wedding celebrations. It was such a brilliant night and Ian and his wonderful wife, Shirley, renewed their vows. Luckily they were written down for him but he did manage a few ad libs. As you entered the Hotel Ryde Castle there was a huge picture of them on their wedding day. One or two of us were still puzzled as to what she actually had seen in him!!

Where do I start? As a schoolboy boxer he was punched on the nose by his cousin and was rushed to hospital. With no ambulance available, he was delivered in an old bread van.

Ian started work as a junior in an Island branch of an Oliver's shoe shop and worked his way up to become a manager. He quickly gained the confidence he'd lacked at Priory Boys School and was promoted to several larger south of England stores and ended up in Croydon. He saw the Brixton riots at close hand and decided to bring Shirley and their three daughters back to the Island.

Becoming a partner in the Ambassador Snooker Club, in Gunville, changed his life for ever. With the sport booming, due to television exposure, they had 12 tables always in action. Later he also opened the Central Park in Newport and had Hurricane Higgins over for a special exhibition.

"When Hurricane had finished, about 1am on the Sunday morning, he fancied a Chinese meal. I told him there was no chance of that in Newport at that time of the morning. He told me it would be okay. I knocked on a Chinese takeaway shop, which had already closed. The manager came down from her flat and could not believe I had Hurricane Higgins with me. She invited us to her upstairs flat and cooked him a special meal. That's fame for you. I just watched – as I don't like Chinese food," said Ian.

He had the Island's first real karaoke machine at a cost of £8000. Many remember Ian's Plaice, his fish and chip shop on Ryde seafront. At weekends his takeaway, that also provided kebabs, opened until 3am.

Ian was also a matchmaker. He ran speed dating sessions at the Countryman, Brighstone and Newport's Riverside Centre. They had 50 at each event, with an equal split. Several marriages evolved from those nights.

Shirley was making a cup of tea in the kitchen, so he opened up a bit. "If they were a man short I would join in and I enjoyed a lot of chatting up. I just wanted to make sure a lady didn't feel lonely, sat on her own."

When Shirley took in some ironing for a few friends in Chillerton, Ian sensed a business opportunity and so Wight Ironing Services was born. It's another success story.

Ian had a special birthday around the time of his golden wedding. I assumed it was his 70th – although several of his pals suggested it was the next big one. How could they! He's too old for Buttons, anyway!

CHAPTER 43

Graham Fenton

I FIRST MET GRAHAM FENTON in the autumn of 1979 when his band, Matchbox, played a gig at the Ponda Rosa, Ashey. At that time, he'd been seen on *Top Of The Pops* singing their rising hit of the time, *Rockabilly Rebel*, and been interviewed on Radio 1. I last saw him perform 39 years later, when he joined original American rock 'n' roll star Charlie Gracie on stage at the Camp Hill Community Club, in late 2018, to sing *Heart Like A Rock*. He may have looked older but he had just as much enthusiasm and love for the music as he had when I first saw him.

Graham has been an Islander now for many years and commutes from his Lake home to Matchbox gigs all around the world. Locally, he's appeared many times at the local Garlic Festival, for Alex Dyke and 'Doc' Holmes. Ironically, back in 1979 when I first interviewed Graham, a young and ambitious Island DJ who wanted to become a radio pop music presenter had never even heard of him. I soon put that right.

Graham's great hero was Gene Vincent and he did get to meet his idol before he died. In fact he saw a lot of him. When Graham was in the House Shakers band, before he joined Matchbox, they actually backed Gene on a European tour. Since then he's actually sung with members of Vincent's old band, The Blue Caps.

Matchbox are still gigging and are so popular in Europe, where they make a few television appearances. Their brand of rockabilly music still has a great following and over the years they have enjoyed several huge hits in Britain and beyond. These include *Midnight Dynamos*, *When You Ask About Love* and *Over The Rainbow/You Belong To Me*. The latter being a medley.

Graham is never asked twice to join another performer on stage and he can produce a picture of himself, with one of his idols, in an instant. Over the years he's performed on numerous bills with some legendary performers. Right back in 1972 the House Shakers appeared in a Wembley rock 'n' roll show alongside Little Richard, Bill Haley, Jerry Lee Lewis, Joe Brown and Billy Fury. The band actually backed Chuck Berry and Bo Diddley. Graham was seen in the film of the concert opening the show in all black performing his tribute spot to Gene Vincent, who had died the previous year.

Going back to that 1979 interview, he told me: "I joined the new Matchbox group in 1977. At the time I was looking for a good band to back me and they had just the sound I wanted."

Like many other British bands, they were ripped off by agents and companies. Once *Rockabilly Rebel* took off they were in business and the proof is in the fact they are still gigging.

Graham Fenton is one of the real nice guys in the music business and is always happy to undertake charity work. In 2015 he was one of those who took part in the 12-hour Riverside rock 'n' roll marathon, in aid of the EM Hospice.

In late 2015 Graham sent me an email during his very successful tour of Japan – and he was excited.

"The fans here know all the words of my songs and I'm getting some great receptions. I've not been here for 35 years and then it was just for television and to record a few songs. I am now finally appearing live for my Japanese fans."

It was a long way from Lake!

CHAPTER 44

Gerry Moglione

"LIFE WAS NOT EASY for a kid growing up in Liverpool. We had a tough neighbourhood and any kid with ears was a tourist," quipped Gerry Moglione, when I interviewed him in 1989. It was all rather different when he moved to the Island in 1966 to become head of PE at my old school, Cowes Secondary Modern. He enjoyed every minute during his ten year stay.

His earliest sporting idol was Billy Liddell the great Liverpool soccer hero – and he played for next to nothing. At school Gerry played football and rugby but was most impressive as a gymnast. At the city's Collegiate College, where he had a scholarship, other pupils included Brian Labone, who went on the play 451 games for Everton, and runner Tom Farrell, who later captained the British Olympic team.

Gerry joined the RAF when he was 18 and served in Germany. After his demob, he went to Westminster College, London and qualified as a teacher. On his eventual return to Liverpool it took him back to his childhood sweetheart. Their lifetime love affair lasted until January of 1989, when she died here of leukaemia. June had played at number one for the Plessey Badminton Club.

"A lot of my ex-pupils called her mum and when she passed away a lot of them rang me up and sent me cards. I appreciated that so much."

Before moving to the Island Gerry had been involved with the Liverpool Boys team and they trained at the Reds training ground with Bill Shankly.

At Cowes Sec he was so proud of his football team and their budding local starlets included Paul Woolford, Gordon Chiverton, Andy Pryke and Mike Hygate.

"I called them all my boys, which made my wife smile," said Gerry.

While at Ward Avenue he also helped young cross country runners like Ian Haslock and Garnet Christophers to great successes and was thrilled when hurdler Janice Stockbridge triumphed in the Hampshire Schools Championships. Between you and me, yours truly had won the mile event a few years earlier.

Gerry has always thrived on hard work in both his career and leisure time. For 14 years he was involved with ocean racing. He began with Sid Cole and ended up on Perseverance with Sir Max Aitken. Squash and golf have also been an enjoyable part of his Island sporting life. His other pursuits have included the Cowes Round Table and the Vectis 41 Club. For six years he was the flight lieutenant of the Cowes Combined Cadet Force.

When Medina High opened Gerry left his PE job at Cowes to teach history there. My wife and I used to meet him at parents nights and it was always such a pleasure and easy to see why he was so liked by pupils.

It's back to Cowes Sec for one of my favourite Gerry Moglione stories. They were returning from a school match on the mainland and on the ferry his team must have thought he looked fed up. Never lost for words Gordon Chiverton told him: " Sir, we've had a whip round to buy you a pint."

In more recent years he's been saddened by the fact that in some cases both students and staff don't want to give up time for sport.

"Sport in schools did such an awful lot to bring teachers and kids together."

During his many years on the Island Gerry has done so much for local youngsters. To all of them he was someone rather special. I sometimes see him shopping in Sainsbury's and love our chats. His advice is always worth listening to.

There is a happy ending, too. He is now married to Margaret.

Those tough Liverpool streets taught him a lot – and he's still got both ears!

CHAPTER 45

John Toogood

FOR MANY YEARS I used to meet John Toogood every Saturday morning in Nodehill, Newport, doing some quick shopping before meeting up with a few of his old pals for a coffee and a chat. Probably about the good old days. I tried to tempt him on to my radio show – and he took quite a lot of persuading. He was nervous but came to life with stories of a few old Newport characters.

When I sat with him at a Wootton wake in early 2019 he told me he had all my first three books and was looking forward to my fourth, which is this one you are reading. I then had an idea but never mentioned it to him. I had one vacant chapter to fill and had several people in mind. I suddenly decided it was going to be him.

John and I initially met when we played football for Parkhurst Old Boys. The first team were virtually unbeatable – so we were mainly in the reserve side. He still loves his soccer and can often be seen at the home matches of Whitecroft and Barton. He always sits in the clubhouse to watch – and has been known to sleep through a few goals.

He has some great old stories of Island life and, one in particular, is worth telling. It involves a guy called Bill West. Charlie Fallick, a friend of his, had, apparently, never been off the Island – and he wasn't a young man. In fact, he never wanted to go to the mainland. Bill took him one day and told him he was on the chain ferry from Cowes to East Cowes. I think he might have wondered why it took so long (that was when it didn't break down) and he was excited to see a train without any smoke coming out. Rumour suggests, he never ever went to the 'north island' again.

John worked on ocean going liners for many years. His first ship was the Union Castle's *Pendennis Castle*, which took three weeks to get to South Africa. They carried cargo and passengers.

When John was on the Cunard ship RMS *Coronia* he was made a lounge steward. It was purely his responsibility – and it was full of very rich and posh people.

"I loved it. I was earning £10 a week. My tips were £150 a week. That would be about £5000 today."

When he was on the *Queen Mary* he met Tommy Cooper and went ashore for a drink with him. His fondest memory was meeting the former world heavyweight champion boxer Jack Dempsey, in a Broadway bar. They had their picture taken together. One of his great passions has always been boxing and during his life John has met Terry Downes, John Conteh and Billy Walker.

John is a former Island boxer and he used to fight at around 10 stone. He stopped one or two of his opponents but suffered from pre-fight nerves, which often meant he lost weight without dieting. He has been involved with the Newport Amateur Boxing Club for many years and served them in many capacities.

When their wooden nissen hut burnt down in 1980, many think by vandals, John designed their brand new building and it was built of brick and could be turned into a house, if the membership dwindled. It never has.

John also loves to fish at Ireland's Dingle Peninsular, where they filmed *Ryan's Daughter*. He even wrote a book about the area. Bernard Cribbins is also a regular visitor and John has seen him there. Probably fishing from a hole in the ground!

John and Anne were also known for their *Forget Me Not* shop. They took over Nodehill Post Office and made it five times larger.

CHAPTER 46

Lord Ronnie Morris

LORD RONNIE MORRIS was one of Ryde's most colourful characters in the 50s and 60s. He led one of the town's most feared gangs and, on one occasion, he took on several professional wrestlers in the Bow Bars, single handed. There were also always rumours about the 'Great Isle of Wight Train Robbery.'

We all knew the reputation of Ronnie Morris – and by the way, he didn't self-impose the Lord in front of his name. He was christened Lord Ronnie Morris.

When he came live on to my IW *Radio* chat show in 1992, the trailer had only been on air for a few minutes before the first complaint came in. It was all good publicity and thousands tuned in. I'd met him and a few of his old gang a couple of days before the show and wondered what the fuss was all about. He was a respectable businessman, had a lovely wife called Liz and a great sense of humour. What I liked about him was the fact that he never tried to pretend his past didn't exist.

Ron did admit to have been a kind of Jekyll and Hyde type of character. Those days had passed and he was then in bed by the time he used to leave for a night on the town.

What about those days of the 50s and 60s, when most local towns had gangs? It just happened that Ronnie's was the most feared.

"Just after the war and into the 50s Ryde was really a fantastic place. With soldiers stationed at Albany, Golden Hill, Sandown and Nettlestone, they were always coming into Newport or Ryde, looking to have a good time, spend their money and pinch our girls. On your own, you didn't stand much of a chance.

"We never robbed anybody, we never mugged anybody, never damaged anyone else's property, took no drugs and no innocent bystanders got hurt." reflected Ronnie.

Some may find it hard to believe but, at the age of seven, Ronnie was an altar boy at St Mary's Catholic School. When he left school he drove the trams on Ryde Pier.

"In those days it was only tuppence and sometimes we got 50,000 visitors a day."

Ronnie also became a local impresario and was the first person to promote the Island's wild rock 'n' roll star Johnny Vincent. He got £5 a night for putting him on. Apparently, most of that went back over the bar and Johnny was lucky to get a pint out of it.

When Vincent entered local talent contests Ronnie and the boys arranged a little extra clapping.

Ronnie loved his local music and told me: "The Cherokees were by far the best at that time. I can even remember that lot in short trousers."

Was there such a thing as the 'Great Isle of Wight Train Robbery'? Did a posse of local lads attempt to halt a Brading to Ryde train, on horseback?

"I can't say one way or the other. It will all be in my book," teased Ronnie. I don't think the book ever came out. I guess the legendary story lives on.

In the late 60s Ronnie became the estate manager for John Lennon, at Tittenhurst, near Ascot. While living in the grounds he met Ringo Starr, George Harrison and Bob Dylan. When they all came to the 1969 Wootton Festival, Ronnie stayed home to look after the estate.

"John Lennon gave me a super diary for my 1969 Christmas present, which was very precious to me. I loaned it to someone and it was stolen," revealed Ronnie. He could have reformed the old gang to get it back – on horseback, perhaps!

Obviously, inspired by Lennon, Ronnie wrote some good songs. He reckoned one would have suited Cliff Richard.

Just a couple of days after the radio show Ronnie took me and Heather out for dinner in Brading. On the way home she remarked what a lovely man he was, so gentle and genial. I did explain it was not quite like that 40 years ago.

CHAPTER 47

Marius Goring

IN MY LIFELONG QUEST to track down as many Isle of Wight-born famous people as I could, in 1985 I headed to the wonderful Kings Theatre, Southsea, to catch the national tour of I Have Been Here Before, ironically, written by a former Islander, JB Priestley. My target was the top movie, stage and television actor Marius Goring, famous for starring in over 70 movies, including O*dette*, I*ll Met By Moonlight*, the all-time classic T*he Red Shoes* and TV's T*he Expert*.

He was born in 1912, in Newport, and was the son of a Parkhurst Prison doctor. At the time his father was writing a book on the English convict. Marius continued to love the Island and often came back to enjoy his favourite haunts. These included Bonchurch and Newtown Creek. In the late 90s his daughter, Phyllida, moved here to St Lawrence and I went to interview her and was made most welcome.

Marius was always going to be an actor. At the age of nine he began to study acting at London's Old Vic School and six years later made his debut on the West End stage. He went on to enjoy a memorable career.

Millions loved his portrayal of Professor John Hardy, the pathologist, in the hit television series called T*he Expert*, which ran from 1968 to 1976. He starred in every one of the 62 episodes.

He told me in Southsea: "That was such a popular BBC series and none of it was fiction. It was based on real-life events. In a way my role as a pathologist was connected with my father's work. The pathology of criminal types."

Marius starred in the massive movie hit T*he Red Shoes*, with Moira Shearer and Anton Walbrook. It won Academy Awards and had so many nominations. Made in 1948 to huge acclaim, it was a worldwide success and Martin Scorsese names it as one of his favourite films of all time. In 1999 it was voted into the top ten of the best British films ever made. It was made for £500,000 and for many years became Britain's highest-earning movie in America. Among his other 70 movies were E*xodus*, D*esert Mice* and T*he Angry Hills*. He also played George V in the massive television series E*dward & Mrs Simpson*.

When we met, he'd been on the stage for over 60 years. What drove him on? Hadn't he seen it all before? It must have been the love of acting to send him around Britain at the age of 73.

"Acting is a sort of extra life that you can switch on and off. Every night at the theatre is like a secret life of one's own."

In over 60 years on the stage he played numerous classic roles, including Ariel in T*he Tempest*, Feste in T*welfth Night* and James I in T*he Wisest Fool*. He still had an ambition to play King Lear. Sadly, this was never achieved before he died in 1998.

Phyllida Goring came to work at Osborne House during her 20 years in the nursing profession. She actually met her husband, Malcolm, at Osborne and they were married in Newport. Her earliest memories included seeing her father playing opposite Vivien Leigh in the West End, sitting next to the British Ambassador during the Paris premiere of her father's movie A M*atter Of Life And Death* and enjoying the occasions Charles Laughton visited their family home.

In 1991 she was so thrilled when Marius was awarded a CBE for services to his profession. Another Islander we can be proud of.

CHAPTER 48

Edana Minghella

THE FIRST TIME I really got to know Edana Minghella was when I went to London in 2005 for the press launch of the second series of the TV hit show *Doc Martin*. Her brother, Dominic, also featured in this book, had invited me to the screening. He created the series and for several of the new episodes he'd been joined by Edana, as his co-writer. I remember sitting between them and hoping I laughed in the right places – and, apparently, I did.

I was surprised a year later to be invited to the Quay Arts Centre, Newport, to see the Island debut of Edana, as a jazz singer. She appeared with her band and impressed everyone in the full house. A lot of planning and thought went into this showcase and it was an evening to savour. I was also privileged to be asked to review it.

A year or two later Edana invited me down to her Brighton home to talk about her debut album and I was able to bring back a special pre-release copy. My trip to Sussex also allowed me to trace her remarkable story.

Initially, Edana went to college to study drama but felt a little uneasy in following in the footsteps of her older brother Anthony.

"He was my great hero and I was a little in awe of him." reflected Edana.

In the end she changed direction completely and trained to become a psychiatric nurse. Jobs were not easy to come by in the late 70s and her love of people and helping to ease their problems created her new goal. Amazingly, her two closest friends, also training with the same dedication, were the now top comedy star and TV presenter Jo Brand and Helen Griffin, who went on to become a top actor and writer. Sadly, she died in 2018.

Edana's job was extremely demanding and at times was not easy to cope with. She worked for five years with suicidal people in the casualty department of King's College Hospital, London.

It was not always easy to leave her problems at work and often meant playing hard, socially, to just chill out. Being in the company of Jo Brand and friends was the perfect remedy.

Later Edana moved into working closely with people who were trying to shape the future of our health industry. For relaxation, she joined a writers circle and had a few short stories published. That led her to leave the industry for a while. She had a head full of plots for *Doc Martin* and even went to the Cornwall locations to see if they would work in the series. Many were influenced by her years in the NHS. One particular story was rather poignant. Her next door neighbour in Brighton suffered from diabetes.

Edana has continued her jazz singing and is always in demand for appearances along the south coast. She has also performed in Italy and released a second album, called *All Or Nothing*.

Since our last interview, in which she hinted about a possible play, she has written one called A *Mother's Song*, for Ten Angry Women. This was performed in the Brighton Dome in 2017. She has hopes for another play, which is now in the development stage, but is not keen to say any more about it. Apparently, it has a really interesting storyline. A novel could be another project but any plans are still in the drawer.

The Minghella family continues to flourish with new and exciting talents. Edana is an aunt to both English actor and screenwriter Max Minghella and his sister, Hannah, the chief of TriStar Pictures. She's been described as one of the coolest people working in Hollywood.

CHAPTER 49

John Howe

JOHN HOWE and his lovely wife, Pat, contacted me back in the 70s looking for some publicity. Thanks to South Wight Council, their Talk of the Wight group were provided with a yearly grant to provide summer entertainment for the West Wight, which gave both locals and visitors the chance to see top class professional shows on their own doorstep.

John contacted me to ask if I would like to come out and interview some of the star names they had booked for the Memorial Hall. I'll never forget those days. I can remember interviewing Joe Brown, Frank Ifield, Marty Wilde, the Tremeloes, with their original line-up, Roy Castle, the Searchers, Helen Shapiro and the Beverley Sisters. I even interviewed the greatest singer in the world – well he told me he was! That could only be Britain's top self-promoter, Jess Conrad. Don't say who? He'd be so upset.

"Our audiences were like a large family and they came time and time again. On occasions they had even booked tickets before they knew who was in the show.

"I loved meeting the stars and most of them were so nice to deal with. Roy Castle was one of the most genuine people we ever had. He even signed many posters that we sold for charity," said John, when I interviewed him a year or two ago.

Everyone remembers the night there was a power cut when Frank Ifield was on stage. He came back to sing with a lightsaber torch.

During those Talk of the Wight days John was working on hovercraft at BHC – and he loved every minute. On show days he would rush home from work to the Memorial Hall to be the main backstage guy at the theatre. I was flattered to introduce a few acts from the wings.

John was born in Shanklin during the second world war, where his grandparents had owned the seafront Broadclyst Hotel. When his father returned from the RAF they moved to the West Wight.

Before arriving at BHC, John had spent a few years in London as an apprentice electrician. Then came spells at a Carisbrooke electrical firm, Thorneycroft's, at Southampton, and Island printers J Arthur Dixon.

Away from the day job and the visiting stars John has always been prepared to work voluntarily for the community. For many years he was one of the drivers for the West Wight's Tennyson ambulance and he also found time for coastguard shifts.

Pat, who sadly died in 2012, always gave John great support. She would enthusiastically ring me up to tell me what stars they had booked for the Memorial Hall.

John with his wife Pat

In 2005 it was such a great shock when John lost his IW Council seat by just a dozen votes. He had worked tirelessly for Totland but was a victim of the mass cull of the Island's sitting Liberals, who had been so unpopular. Sanity was restored in 2009 when he won back his seat.

John has not been a publicity minded councillor and has never sought local paper headlines or radio station sound bites. He just gets on with the job and enjoys every minute.

I've known him for over 40 years and it's always such a pleasure to meet up with him. He's a real people person. I've admired his love of family life, his work ethic, unassuming attitude and a genuine care for other people.

There was only one occasion when I couldn't talk to him. It was the night the Merseybeats came to Freshwater. They must have heard them on the Needles.

CHAPTER 50

Mark Wyndham-Jones

I INTERVIEWED Mark Wyndham-Jones on several occasions and the one I remember the most vividly was when he came in as a live guest on Sunday February 17, 1991. He couldn't believe it. He arrived at the studio at around noon and found he was on the same live show as the Beverley Sisters. It might not have done his street cred any favours with his pals in the Hurricanes rugby team but he loved every minute and Joy, Teddie and Babs made such a fuss of him.

In the late 70s Mark, who had played football for Sandown and Brading, became totally disillusioned with the Island game and he opted to play rugby for the Sandown and Shanklin RFC, known to many as the Hurricanes.

Why had he made this shock move? "With the many suspensions I used to incur and the games continually off for bad weather I just got fed up. Strikers were never protected by the referees. As a forward in rugby you're involved for the full 80 minutes and get no time for tantrums. You can get rid of all your aggression in just one tackle."

He only started playing rugby during his suspensions from soccer. It was a completely new ball game for him. He told me: "Anyone can get a game at a certain level of rugby, even if they're 18 stone or four foot tall. The fitter and stronger you are the better it is."

Mark will never forget his first game of rugby, back in 1976. He played in a Hurricanes team that lost 78-0. Little did he imagine that 12 years later he would skipper the first fifteen in the greatest season in their history. They reached the semi-final of the Hampshire Cup. They had beaten Portsmouth in a previous round, which had shell shocked their more senior opponents.

During his football days, in one Hampshire League season for Sandown he scored 29 goals. He liked Sunday soccer, too. Once, his aggregate for two consecutive games reached an astonishing 20 goals. Sometimes, after a rugby season, he went to Brading for a few games of football.

When Mark left the Island I lost contact with him, which was a disappointment because he is such good company. Then out of the blue I got an email from him and we were able to meet up again at the Hurricanes clubhouse in the summer of 2018. We hadn't met up since it was Mark Wyndham-Jones and the Beverley Sisters. What a supergroup that could have been!

Mark has always been a fanatical trainer and has kept fit all of his life – and it's still continuing. He lives a lot now in New Zealand and at the age of 65 decided to take athletics more seriously. He won his first-ever decathlon and some of the other athletes called him 'The Invisible Man' and asked "where the f--- has he come from."

He kept on winning medals and, after just 18 months of competitions, came seventh in the World Championships in Malaga.

"I decided I didn't want to become one of those old boys who just sat in a pub. I could have been but I'm glad I didn't."

I'll never forget when he became the Bevs Mr Wonderful for an hour, back in 1991. That song could have been written for him. A few ex-Island soccer referees might not have thought so – and probably not his New Zealand decathlon rivals.

CHAPTER 51

Miff Mowle

THERE WAS NO MISTAKING the Island's Miff Mowle. He was hairless, drove an original 1966 green Spitfire sports car and was mainly seen blowing a pretty hot saxophone. His life story included Shirley Bassey, Peggy Lee, Tony Bennett, Victor Borge, Ginger Baker and Jack Bruce.

Following his RAF days, when he became a full time service musician, back in civvy street he became a freelance musician. He spent four years in Nairobi and then came back to England to play in the Jack Nathan Orchestra. They played a mammoth stint at London's famous Pigalle Club and backed top stars like Betty Hutton and Patti Page.

Miff once told me: "When we played for Peggy Lee she gave us all a gas cigarette lighter with our initials on."

He appeared on the album *Shirley Bassey At The Pigalle* and was in her backing orchestra at the 1965 Royal Variety Performance.

Jack Nathan gave Miff time off to work on the cruise liners and in holiday camp bands. In the mid 1950s the Island's best band was at the Brambles Chine holiday park, fronted by Bill Findlay. They brought London's star musicians down for their summer season. That was when Miff fell in love with the Island. During one season the legendary musician and broadcaster Benny Green played alongside Miff.

He went back to London for the winter seasons and played in the jazz-styled Johnny Burch Octet. Their personnel included Jack Bruce, Ginger Baker, Graham Bond and Dick Heckstall-Smith.

"Jack and Ginger were great fun but were fed up not making much money playing jazz. That all changed when they formed Cream a year or two later," said Miff.

Eventually Miff moved here and settled in Ryde. He was also known for cycling all over the Island. When he had the Miff Mowle Quartet on the cruise liners he would also take his fold-up bike to countries all around the world. For a while he played with local musicians on the high seas, including Tim Marshall, Doug Watson and Alan Dale. In 1975 he'd been in the band on the QE2's first world cruise.

Miff also did summer seasons here at Norton Chalet Hotel, Little Canada, Woodside Bay and Nodes Point. He was in the Sandown Pavilion Orchestra for seasons with Dickie Henderson, Cilla Black and Billy Dainty. Being in the locally acclaimed Bob Howarth Big Band was also a special moment in his long career.

The last time I met Miff was in 1999 when I did an article on him for the *County Press*. This was just before he moved to France. His last Island gig was at a New Year's Eve dance at the Royal York Hotel, Ryde, with the Mike Nash Band.

What was the reasoning behind his move? "The Island traffic is now so horrendous and in France it's so much easier for cyclists and the motorists are so considerate," was his answer. He did come back a few times to see old friends but died in France.

Miff had so many stories to tell and like numerous band musicians had a huge capacity for liquid refreshment.

He once told me about one of the greatest experiences of his life. His idol, Count Basie, was on board the QE2 for a short stint. Miff met him and even sat in on a jam session with some of the Basie band.

CHAPTER 52

Mick Bull

MICK BULL LOVED reporting on Island football. When some of his old colleagues were at home on winter Saturday afternoons watching black and white movies or the latest scores from the big matches, he was still standing on exposed local pitches, without a stand in sight, reporting Island League matches in cold and damp conditions. It certainly was for the love of the games and not the money.

We'd known each other since our days on the *Weekly Post*. They produced the best Island sports coverage ever seen in a local paper. Mick also became a household name for his Bullseye darts column. In 1993 I decided it was about time he was interviewed for a local paper and he became my Sports Personality in the *Island Times*.

Mick also came live into my IW *Radio* Sunday lunchtime show and, sadly, was there the day we were phoned to say the much-loved Tony Best had died earlier that morning. That unexpected news quickly changed the mood of the footballers who were in the studio.

Mick's schoolboy sporting prowess had been non existent. Attending a convent school in Shanklin gave him no opportunity. His first job was at J Arthur Dixon's and he played a few friendly soccer games for them. That led to Island League soccer as a left winger for Rookley Blue Star and then he had spells at Newchurch and Shanklin.

"I was such an unconfident footballer. Unless you really believe in yourself, the other person will always be better."

In 1963, when he moved to the Isle of Wight Times, at Lightbown's, the Ryde printers, he watched the all-conquering Binstead team. Mac Richards asked him to write a few words about their matches and it all took off from then. He was also grateful for the encouragement from their editor Clive Barton.

He discovered Seaview FC almost by accident. He went on the Shanklin coach, he lived near their ground, to a match at Seagrove Bay. They had a star-studded team and were managed by the legendary Roy Shiner. Their games with Saro, Brading, Parkhurst and West Wight were worth going miles to see.

"Players like Barry Allen, Tony Grimwade, Nobby Nash and Oscar Stretch made excellent copy. The football was so much better in those days. With Oscar, it was a story if he was not booked or sent off."

Mick's darts column was the bible for hundreds of local fans. At that time people like Roger Mazillius, John Young and Martin Humphray did so much for Island darts.

Later Mick covered Ryde Sports, when they had a very indifferent team. Luckily, he was also able to cover the rising success of Newport Football Club but did miss the amazing atmosphere of their old Church Litten ground, after they moved to St George's Park.

In 1998 Mick struck gold on the day Vinnie Jones played virtually on his own doorstep, in a special celebration match at Shanklin Football Club. The notorious Wimbledon player got into real trouble and was sent off for striking a local postman. *The Sun* newspaper got a whiff of the story and phoned the Shanklin Football Club. The clubhouse suggested they rang Mick, who was at the game. It was a hot story and he got a wee bit more money than he did writing for the *Weekly Post* or the *County Press*.

I asked him which was the best game he had ever seen on the Island. I knew the answer before I asked the question – because I was at the same match.

"It must be the epic Seaclose battle between Parkhurst and Seaview. A thousand saw it and two thousand have told me they were there. It's still a growing legend."

Just for the record Seaview won 7-6.

Mick's books on local football have all been best sellers.

CHAPTER 53

Maurice Keat

THE FIRST TIME I ever met Maurice Keat was at Westwood Park, the home of Cowes Football Club. It was at the final of the Primary League Championship. We were the opposing goalkeepers. He was in goal for Cowes Denmark Road and I was in goal for East Cowes Grange Road. They beat us 2-0 and I was much busier than he was. I had been off school with German measles but was allowed to play. It proved my finest performance as a schoolboy goalkeeper. When we moved to Cowes Secondary Modern we were rivals for the goalkeepers jersey. I just managed to keep him out.

When we met up again 23 years later Maurice just blew me away. He was a superb professional musician in the Royal Marines – and I just couldn't play a note. At that time he was the director of music for the Ryde Concert Band, the IW Youth Concert Band and the County Wind Band.

Maurice had left Cowes Secondary and moved across the river to the East Cowes Technical School. He played in their orchestra and was a member of the Cowes Salvation Army Band. Music became both his life and career.

Initially, he'd endured a very sad early life. He lost both parents and a brother in the war and another brother had died in a fire. His grandmother, who brought him up, encouraged him to play music. Maurice owes her such a lot.

At the age of 16 he joined the Royal Marines as a junior musician and was posted to Deal. This entailed 18 months training and playing music up to 12 hours a day. He assured me he did find time to be successful in the depot's soccer and cricket teams.

"I joined as a cornet player but they were much too good for me and after six months I moved to a French horn," said Maurice.

His first assignment as a full time professional musician came with a visit to Singapore, where he played in the Commander in Chief's Band, which contained 24 musicians. After his exploits in the sun he came back to HMS *Excellent* in Portsmouth for four years. Pompey proved lucky for him, as he met his lovely wife Terri.

Within the world of services music, Maurice became the youngest ever corporal and then a few years later the youngest ever sergeant. His music took him to Dartmouth, Plymouth, Deal and back to Portsmouth. He became bandmaster at HMS *Daedalus*. On one occasion he presented a 120-strong band on Southsea Common for the Fleet Review. He spent 24 years in the Marines.

Back on the Island, so many young people and more experienced musicians were helped in so many ways by Maurice. He was a tough taskmaster and really put them through their paces.

When Maurice was 14 he'd played in the Ryde ATC Band. Later he came back to be their director of music. It was then called the Ryde Concert Band. They were even seen in the hit television series *Duchess Of Duke Street*.

"That was great publicity for us and the royalties were great for our funds. The series was sold to many countries."

Maurice also had great success with the IW Youth Concert Band, under the auspices of the Bembridge Young Community Club and the wonderful Ray Rowsell. They toured the world and, nearer to home, enjoyed brilliant local sell-out concerts. These included movie themes, songs from hit musicals and pop songs.

Hundreds of Island youngsters owe so much to the musical talents of Maurice Keat – and he was not a bad goalie either. Apparently, he's been known to play golf!

Andy King

I FIRST INTERVIEWED Andy King in the summer of 1981. It was quite a change to produce a notebook in front of one of the most notorious football referees on the Island. He'd waved a few in front of me when I was playing football for Parkhurst. At that time he'd taken charge of 1800 games. Neither of us could ever have imagined that he'd still be refereeing 38 years later. You could fill many chapters in this book by just listing the names of players he's booked or sent off since he began in 1957.

Andy lived in Niton and his great aunt introduced him to football. She took him on away trips with the local team and then his father took him to Fratton Park in the great days of Dickinson and Froggatt. There were 40,000 present. He went back a few years later as a linesman in a Hampshire Junior A cup final and this time there were the two teams, the three officials and a few seagulls.

Unofficially, he took his first match at the age of 14. He should have been 15. It was a local derby between Ventnor Reserves and Wroxall. It proved to be the expected battle and our young Andy gave four penalties.

August 28, 1957, was his day to remember. He was 15 years and one day and refereed the Niton v Binstead game. The visitors won 10-0.

"I was very meek and mild in those days but you didn't need to be strong. There were no obscenities or violence," said Andy.

I find this hard to believe but he never booked a single player during his first five years. Things did change!

Today's social media brigade would have had a field day when Andy refereed a game between Apse Heath and J S Whites Reserves. The visitors coach driver was their linesman and at the end of the game he chased Andy across the pitch. He kept running, grabbed his own bike from under the hedge and never stopped pedalling until he reached Wroxall.

Andy became a very strong referee with a no-nonsense attitude and his reputation spread like wildfire. His progress was being monitored and he was earmarked for promotion to a higher grade of soccer. An assessor was present at a match in Fareham when Andy sent a player off but he wouldn't go or give his name. He remained cool and got promotion.

In 1968 he was asked about taking games in the Football Combination, for the reserve teams of Football League clubs. When he was asked if he could do any match, he had to reply with a no. Work commitments for the local Post Office made it difficult for him to travel. Today it would have been easier when youngsters, like our own Lee Probert and James Linington, can make a career in the game.

Has he been book happy during his long career?

"I have always tried to referee to the book. No-one can complain about the things I have cautioned or sent them off for. I have never made up my own laws. I am sorry some other referees don't follow my policy. If players start the rough stuff, I sort them out." He made that comment in '81 – and has continued to maintain that policy. Good for him.

Like quite a few others, I think Andy could have become a top referee, if times had been different. What he has done in recent years is to put such a lot back into the game with his admirable jobs in local football administration. Many would run away from what he's taken on – and made a success of.

CHAPTER 55

Alan Taylor

BERNIE CULLEN PHONED to tell me he'd met a very interesting guy in a Newport pub and I should talk to him. I went to this small flat in the centre of the town and was amazed. Alan Taylor's story includes Cary Grant, Tina Turner, Nelson Mandela, Dave Young and Joe Reed. He also grew up in my hometown of East Cowes.

When he was a 14 year old schoolboy he'd helped local coalman Charlie Hodge. A few years earlier he'd been a paperboy for Godsland's newsagents,

"We used to play in the old East Cowes Castle, which was in a very bad state. We would lower the thinnest boy down the huge chimney stack, with a rope around his legs, to get at the crows' nests," said Alan.

He also played football for East Cowes Vics, with guys like Dave Young and Joe Reed. At JS White's Shipyard he began as their internal postman, with a green container on his bike. He did admit his wheeler-dealer father, Jock, who also worked in the shipyard, sometimes gave him extra freight to smuggle out. Usually cigarettes from visiting ships.

After becoming an apprentice welder, Alan moved on to Bristol and began work on the SS *Great Britain*. There, by sheer good luck, he saw one of the most famous faces in the world. It was Hollywood icon Cary Grant, who was making a return visit to his home city.

"I was in my scruffy working clothes but welcomed Mr Grant and I asked him if I could take a couple of snaps. I always had my Box Brownie camera in my work cupboard. He was friendly, asked my name and said yes.

"Being the only photographer around and with him being such a world famous star, I was able to send the pictures all around the world. I quickly learned a lesson. When you are dealing with the press get your money first."

Meeting Cary Grant was indeed an affair to remember. It directly led to Alan becoming a freelance photographer. In 1974 he got the chance of a lifetime – the opportunity to go to South Africa with the British Lions rugby team. He instantly fell in love with the country and made some important contacts.

"In the end I decided to go over there and live. Over here I was a nobody but over there I had all my contacts and could produce good photographs."

For many years he worked for the *Cape Times*. His pictures also appeared in *Time Magazine*. He took shots of top pop stars like Tina Turner and Bono. After a photo shoot at Nelson Mandela's home, he was invited to stay for lunch. The great man even phoned Alan's office to tell them he'd be late. His boss thought it was a wind-up.

"I didn't like all I saw over there and my eyes were quickly opened to apartheid. I had never seen segregation between human beings. When you walked down the streets the black people moved off the pavements and said sorry. I wanted to have a drink with black working friends but was not allowed to."

Several of his close friends lost their lives covering stories. Once, after being fired on by tear gas, Alan awoke to find a small Zulu boy standing over him and washing him with water. He particularly enjoyed the Zulu people.

Alan, who returned to the Island because of a family illness, did have a South African girlfriend, who later became his wife, and she was registered as black, but at one time they had to keep their meetings secret. If they had been found together, he might never have been around to reveal his amazing story. It was a long way from South Bank Road in East Cowes.

CHAPTER 56

Arnold Olive

I HAVE SEEN thousands of games of football in my lifetime, from Wembley Stadium to the old Oakfield tip, where rusty tins sometimes became visible protruding through the pitch. I can still recall the hardest shot I have ever seen in a match – and this was at Westwood Park, Cowes. It was scored by a local guy called Arnold Olive. It was a Cowes v Newport local derby and the Yachtsmen won 4-1. Newport had a top Navy goalkeeper called Hughes – and he never moved an inch as the ball went by him like a rifle bullet. Big Arn had struck again.

Arnie, another who could score goals just for fun, netted around 1100 in local football. It might have been considerably less, if Portsmouth Football Club had not changed their manager. In one season Arnie scored 120 goals for Oakfield. He was spotted by a Pompey scout, Fred Forward, and invited to Fratton Park for a trial. He played for Portsmouth Reserves and scored a hat trick. This impressed the watching Pompey boss Eddie Lever and he offered Arnie a professional contract. His next decision, indirectly, was to end that dream.

"Eddie asked me to sign as a professional footballer there and then. I was keen but asked if I could see the season out with Oakfield, as they were in with a chance of winning several trophies. I agreed to sign during the summer.

"He liked my loyalty and agreed to the idea. That summer he got the sack and Freddie Cox took over – and he didn't want me," said Arnie, during one of our many interviews. I even managed to persuade him to appear on my television chat show.

Reg Reynolds, the Cowes Football Club secretary, softened his disappointment a little by signing him as a semi professional for the Hampshire League club. That season, in a higher class of soccer, he banged in 42 goals. He formed a great goalscoring partnership with the unforgettable Ash Wingham.

I once asked him who was his first football mentor – and had quite a shock at his reply. "It was my mother. When I was about 11 she told me to hit the ball as hard as I could for the middle of the goal. No-one can kick straight, so it would swerve."

Arnie's wonderful mother also made another major decision in his early life. He was also a gifted boxer and had won the Hampshire schools title.

"I broke my hand winning the Hampshire title and the night before my Southern Counties final it was still in plaster up to my elbow. My mum, who was boxing mad, cut the plaster off and said I was fit to fight the next day in Maidenhead. She was right, as I won it."

Away from the ring and the soccer field, Arnie could certainly take care of business. He was local nightclub doorman and no-one argued with him. Sometimes he was called to London by Wilf Pine, who was employed by Don Arden.

Just a few days before Arnie passed away at the Kite Hill Nursing Home, I went down to cheer him up and talk about the old days. Quite a few of his soccer pals like Brian Morey, Nobby Nash and Bert Cronin also popped in.

He could still vividly remember the night, at Lakeside Inn, when he and a few mates threw local rock 'n' roll star Johnny Vincent into Wootton Creek, just minutes before he was due on stage. I don't think he sang *Splish Splash* that night!

I felt so privileged to be asked to do the eulogy at Arnie's funeral. He was another of my local football heroes. He was actually born in Bolton and, before moving to the Island, went to the same primary school as Tommy Lawton and Nat Lofthouse. What a front line those three would have made.

CHAPTER 57

Anthony Bate

DURING THE AFTERNOON of May 8, 1945, Anthony Bate and his family ended a great adventure by crossing the Solent, en route from Worcestershire, to a new home on the Island. He just couldn't understand the welcome. There were boats everywhere and they were raising flags, flashing lights and sounding sirens, amid great celebrations. The Bate family arrival corresponded with VE Day.

Within three weeks of settling in Shanklin, to help run the family hotel, he was called up for his national service. After three years Anthony's parents took over Seaview's Northbank Hotel. Suddenly his career looked much more promising. He'd hated working in a bank, which was his first real job after leaving school.

I first met him in 1992, in St Helens, and he reflected on those Seaview days.

"It seemed a nice attractive business and I quickly learnt everything from waiting and cooking to preparing some nifty cocktails."

A visit to Watson Brothers grocery store, now sadly missed, was to completely change his life. He was chatted up by the owner's daughter.

"I was minding my own business when she suddenly approached me. I was surprised when she asked me if I wanted to join the local Bellevue Players, who were looking for a young man to play a certain part. I'd never thought about acting and agreed to think about it. She was very attractive, so I agreed."

During the next two years he appeared in six of their productions. His first role was in *Jane Steps Out* and his others included *Mrs Moonlight*, *Dangerous Corner* and *I've Been Here Before*.

His appearance in the IW Drama Festival caught the eye of the London adjudicator and she tempted him to audition for the Central School of Dramatic Art.

"I was accepted but had no money. Being an ex-serviceman, I wrote to Newport Council and got a grant. I was so grateful to them."

During their summer breaks he came back to work in the Seaview hotel. At Central he won high praise for his acting skills, which was such a boost. He'd never been praised during his school days.

His first repertory summer season was in Worthing and then he came to Shanklin Theatre for the Barry O'Brien company. His sister lived in the town, so he got cheap digs. He was only on £8 a week but made enough to marry Diana Watson.

In the mid 50s he made his television debut and never looked back. Many remember him for his starring role in the hit series *Intimate Strangers*. Then came *Tinker Tailor Soldier Spy*, *Smiley's People*, *An Englishman's Castle*, *Game Set And Match*, *Midsomer Murders*, *Silent Witness* and *A Touch Of Frost*. His movies included *Act Of Murder*, *Ghost Story*, *Eminent Domain* and *Give My Regards To Broad Street*, which starred Paul McCartney. On stage he appeared in so many hit West End plays.

Anthony was another actor to emerge from the amateur ranks and become a top and well respected professional. The amazing combination of VE Day, the Isle of Wight, Miss Diana Watson and the Bellevue Players proved an irresistible combination for Anthony Bate.

The last time we met he told me: "I found the Bellevue Players a very positive, stimulating and exciting experience. They awakened senses in me that I never knew I had."

Anthony, who died at St Mary's Hospital in 2012, was such a lovely man. There was never a hint of any kind of ego. I've often wondered what he was really sent to Watson Brothers shop for. He certainly never expected to find a wife or a career in acting.

CHAPTER 58

Charles (Roger) Burden

THE FIRST TIME I ever saw Charles Burden, known affectionately to his friends as Roger, was at the Sandown Pavilion opening night of Holiday Spectacular, in the summer of 1978. He was part of a double act called Burden and Moran, who were billed as Maids of Mystery and Masters of Illusion. In other words, they were a female impersonation duo who presented superb illusions. After the show I met Roger, without his wig and makeup, and he looked the spitting image of Elton John.

A month or two after their opening night, I approached them with regard to a possible interview for the IW *Weekly Post*. They were up for it and agreed to make me up as a drag queen. It would be top secret and was the first time they had allowed this to happen. In past years they had turned down other similar requests.

I had the lot – wig, false eye lashes, lipstick, beauty spots and other womanly aids. Obviously, it took a long time and Charles and Maurice were very strict. Amidst their cries of "don't open your eyes yet" and "mind that lipstick" I had a constant throbbing from my huge ear rings. I kept thinking I wish it was the next day, with just a splash of 'Henry Cooper' after my morning shower.

The big test came when one of the world's top ventriloquists, Arthur Worsley, one of the stars of the show, came into the dressing room. We had become firm friends and he'd been to my home for afternoon tea. He didn't have a clue who I was and kept saying "I know your face from somewhere."

I have been friendly with Charles since that Sandown summer season. He's also got the best selection of coloured and patterned men's shoes I have ever seen and they are all stored in their original boxes. When he goes on holiday he takes 14 pairs of shoes to match his evening attire. I once went to a local showbiz funeral and saw his wonderful purple Italian winkle pickers. The next day I ordered a pair from Gucinari.

Charles fell in love with the Island and moved here permanently in 1979. Now he only leaves for holidays and to play dame in pantomimes. For five years Burden and Moran starred in summer seasons at Shanklin's Westhill Manor.

I was lucky enough to review his 50th pantomime appearance for *The Stage* newspaper. He was Nurse Glucose in *Sleeping Beauty* at the Anvil Theatre, Basingstoke. Burden and Moran were panto favourites but when Maurice, who played a dame, sadly died in 1994, Charles took over the dame role and has never looked back. He's played in over 20 shows for UK Productions.

Back to my 1978 makeover at Sandown Pavilion. After the cameras were put away they left me to it and suggested I went home to face my wife and children. They finally relented and with a quick unzip and a rub of magic potion my new found womanhood was washed away. By the way – I'm not available for panto!

Charles Burden, John Hannam and Maurice Moran

CHAPTER 59

Barrie Millership

I'VE INTERVIEWED so many brilliant bass players with Island connections, including Jet Harris, Mark King, John Illsley, Tim Marshall, Paul Armfield and Keith Roberts. I was also fascinated to meet another, Barrie Millership, who played bass in the legendary Island 60s band The Shamrocks, who were based (sorry about the pun) in Ventnor. I can remember buying a copy of their original German vinyl album, which Barrie was on.

I knew the name Millership, as in my young days I called on the top newsagents in Sandown, which was called Millership's. I knew the father then but not his son Barrie.

When I finally met Barrie it was so good to catch up on the band's fame in Germany and update his own career. Then came his amazing hardback book called *The Mighty Hybrid And The Keeper Of The Slabs*. No it wasn't a crime thriller – it was the story of his 1966 order for a Fender Telecaster Bass. Such a fascinating read. Superbly produced and with stunning photographs.

In 1964 Barrie was a founder member of the Island's Midnight Creepers, with other locals like Chris Mew and Doug Watson. Their first-ever gig was the Savoy Dive Bars in Sandown. Their other hot spots included the Atherfield Bay Holiday Camp and Atlantic Ballroom, Lake.

Later that year Barrie was headhunted by Gary Cowtan, the bass player from the Shamrocks. He was going to concentrate on singing and mouth harp and they wanted Barrie to play bass.

"I went on their first tour of Germany and played bass on their debut album, which was recorded in Berlin. Luckily we became so popular and were constantly mobbed by fans," reflected Barrie.

Their full personnel consisted of Bern Roberts, Pete Channing, Dave Eaglen and Gary and Barrie. This is not quite the place to exploit some of their European adventures. I'll tell you one – but don't tell Barrie. These are his words – not mine.

"We were in a German hotel early one morning when half a dozen pretty girls invaded our rooms. The giggling bevy stripped down to bras and panties and I watched open-eyed as a devastating red-headed beauty coolly removed her clothes and lay down beside me," said Barrie. For some reason, he ended the story there.

One of their greatest gigs was to support the Troggs and Los Bravos in the Vienna Town Hall. There were 12,000 fans at the gig.

Barrie eventually moved on to play in several top British blues bands of the era. One of these was the famous Dr K's Blues Band. In that group was Ashley Hutchings, who became a folk legend by forming groups like Fairport Convention, Steeleye Span and the Albion Band.

After years of playing bass Barrie finally came back to his roots and now lives in Seaview. It was there that he introduced me to his ex-Shamrocks pal Gary Cowtan, who was back on the Island for a nostalgic holiday. He'd stayed on in Germany and produced hit records in his own studio.

Back to the book. I must admit I never expected to be enthralled by the story of a missing Fender Telecaster Bass. Surely a bass guitar was just that. Don't you believe it. I was hooked before the end of the preface. I got very excited when the near 30 year search seemed to be reaching a climax. The missing bass once belonged to a certain Barrie Midford-Millership.

CHAPTER 60

Bob Ennis

I LOVE LISTENING to Bob Ennis – if I'm not in a hurry. He can chat about Island railways, Anthony Minghella, home movies, John Huntley, holiday parks, old movies, television shows and even playing jazz with Terry Lightfoot. I had a few hours to spare in 2018 and was invited to his home to see the first copy of a book he'd dreamed about publishing for years. What a surprise I had. It's a remarkable piece of work called *Shadows Of Magic*. It deserves to be read by a wide audience.

I first met Bob when he and his lovely wife, June, owned the Field Lane Holiday Park at St Helens. They are both perfectionists and ran a top quality small complex and built up a regular clientele of holidaymakers.

I first interviewed Bob in 1985, to tie in with the premiere of his super 8 railway movie *Terrier To Wootton*. This was filmed entirely on the Havenstreet line over nine weekends in the summer months. They were very helpful and kept the train formation the same during his filming weekends. It was a full house for the premiere at the Monday night meeting of the IW Cine Society, which my late father had been involved with many years earlier. Some of my father's railway home movies are still around and can be seen online.

With Bob being a railway buff and a very skilled film maker it was the perfect combination to make this great little movie. He actually began making films in 1941 and has never lost his enthusiasm. He's also marched along with the amazing technical advances of videos, DVDs, high quality cameras, digital recorders and the computer revolution. Alongside these more contemporary inventions he has a brilliant mini museum of old home movie projectors and cameras. I'm not sure that June shares Bob's enthusiasm in the same sort of way

Since *Terrier To Wootton* Bob has made so many fascinating films, many about the Island, which are still available on DVD.

For many years he was thrilled to be involved with the cinema nights at Newport's Medina Theatre, where they had a brilliant sound system. The highlights were when they held the Anthony Minghella movie premiere nights and our late Oscar winner would make the trip and locals dressed up for a night at the Medina. Several charities also benefitted from those special events. Bob was, quite rightly, proud of his friendship with Anthony.

On another occasion Bob came into a special radio programme I did on the history of Island cinemas. At that time his Medina Theatre cinema nights were just going to show *The Living Picture Show*. Before Bob spoke about that, he surprised us with a few facts he'd recently found out.

"It seems the first moving pictures ever seen on the Island were at The Isle of Wight Pavilion at Ventnor, in September 1896. It's almost 100 years to the day that we are putting on *The Living Picture Show* at the Medina Theatre."

That was not all. Bob had also unearthed a story that one of the true all-time greats of world cinema had visited the Island.

"Legend says that Walt Disney had a hate of flying and he used to come to Southampton on the Curnard liners. He then used to sneak off to the Island because he had a love of railways. He would ride on our trains incognito," revealed Bob.

Sadly, the Medina Movie Theatre had to close and so did the wonderful Screen Deluxe in Lake. The power of the huge companies with their multi-screen complexes proved too much to cope with. Thankfully, the brilliant *Talking Pictures* television channel is now a gem for real movie buffs.

CHAPTER 61

Charlie Brook

WHEN I JOINED IW *Radio* in 1990 there was a particularly nice young guy called Charlie Brook working at the station. He made the tea, delivered their car stickers, wrote the travel news and helped tune-in potential listeners. He'd left Holton's, the Shanklin upholsterers, to seek a career in the broadcasting media. The minute he'd seen Philip Schofield in the BBC Children's TV broom cupboard he knew that was all he ever wanted to do.

Within nine years he'd become a popular IW Radio presenter, interviewed Cher, Robbie Williams and Boyzone, produced the chart-topping *In The Mix* albums and shows for Radio 1. He'd also broadcast on *Plymouth Sound Radio* and made shows for CBTV. Charlie had a recurring dream of one day being seen on national television. A few of us knew he would definitely make it. From the moment he began to produce *John Hannam Meets*, I knew he had the technical skills to match his great personality.

In the year 2000 he was seen by millions all over Europe on QVC. He was approached by the shopping channel and obtained the job from 2000 other hopefuls.

"I didn't apply for the job and was not too worried about the auditions, which was unlike me. I was probably a little blasé but I was offered the job," said Charlie, at the first of our interviews for the *County Press* and IW *Radio*.

Charlie made such a charismatic impact on the station and was soon getting fan mail from Great Britain, the Canary Islands, Germany and Scandinavia.

It was the hardest television work he'd undertaken during his career. Being live for three hours in front of the viewers, with no script or autocue, was so demanding. He was simply handed an A5 sheet with a few key notes and then had to improvise and sell to the public.

He told me: "I'm not really a sales person. I just try and be myself." That was the key to his success – just being the Charlie Brook we all love.

Charlie has become a kind cult figure on QVC and his fan club continues to grow. There have been several television moments to savour – like the day he was demonstrating a long tube and got stuck in it. One of his priceless moments.

I was twice invited to the QVC studios, near the Battersea Power Station, to interview Charlie. They were both memorable days. He had his own dressing room with a television, telephone and computer.

On-screen Charlie always looks – to coin an old phrase – as if he's just walked out of Burton's window. He's always beautifully groomed but firmly denies my suggestion his hands are manicured. He often works with QVC's popular Diamonique range and his hands are constantly shown in close up. Charlie – I wasn't born yesterday. They were never like that when he made me a cup of tea at Dodnor Park.

Charlie is a great professional. However, there have been moments when this has been put to the test. Like the evening he was presenting a show out of doors and was attacked by a giant moth and on another occasion when he bravely tasted sliced raw onions on a cooking programme – and wished he hadn't.

I occasionally run into Charlie on a ferry coming back to the Island. He comes home as often as possible to visit his family in Seaview. Thankfully, he's still the same Charlie Brook who was loved by thousands of IW Radio listeners. No ego and just full of fun. I never shake his hand anymore – just in case I ruin his nail varnish!!

CHAPTER 62

Billy Reid Junior

WHEN I FIRST MET Bill Reid, in a Cowes flat overlooking the harbour, he'd previously been delivering bread but had given it up. The job hadn't inspired him in any way. Probably few of his colleagues at Island Bakeries had ever known of his amazing pedigree. That changed, overnight, as he finally decided to reveal his story in my *Weekly Post* Stage Talk column. His late father was world famous songwriter Billy Reid. His songs had been recorded by Frank Sinatra, Ella Fitzgerald, Al Jolson, Nat King Cole, Eddie Fisher, Peggy Lee, Al Martino and Bing Crosby.

In 1988 Bill had finally decided to come clean about his illustrious heritage. This certainly surprised his few close friends. He had the reputation of being a rather shy recluse. His world had suddenly changed. With a new zest for performing, he was fronting his own trio three times a week and writing great songs. What a voice, too! He could swing like any of the top crooners. I still have some of his demo records to prove it.

Bill told me back in August 1988: "Last November I was really on my last legs, until John Wroath picked me up. I just don't know where my determination has come from."

His father, who had also fronted a world famous accordion band, spent some of the last few years of his life in a seafront bungalow at Gurnard. He died in 1974. Bill's mother, Jane, was a very gifted singer. Rumours had always suggested Beryl Reid was Bill's mother, which was way off course. Her popular radio characters of Monica and Marlene couldn't sing anywhere near as well as the Island's Mrs Reid, known originally as Jane Gordon.

Billy Reid's most famous songs were *The Gypsy*, *Tree In A Meadow* and *It's A Pity To Say Goodnight*.

"My father was a genius. He was often called the English Irving Berlin. After dad died I went to London for a while and met people who had known him. That's when I started to find out how good he really was."

Bill wrote his first song at the age of 21 – after a broken romance. He told me: "You have to be on a low to write good songs. That one was called *The Morning* and it's still good."

Billy Reid Junior with, inset, his father

In the early 80s Bill had spent three years in London trying to break in as a songwriter and it was tough. A bad manager didn't help.

"People like Ian Dury and Alex Harvey really liked what I was doing. Unfortunately, I was always being compared to my father and I wanted to make it on my own."

People in the Cowes area were so lucky to witness the talents of Bill Reid. At the time we first met his Bill Reid Band consisted of himself on vocals and guitar, Richard Wilkinson on drums and Roger Burrows on sax. He always included dad's *The Gypsy* in his repertoire. The band also cut a very popular local record, called *Let's Celebrate*.

Bill had real moments of enthusiasm and positive dreams but lacked the confidence to really see them through. On one particular day I visited him in north Hampshire. He'd moved there from the Island and so wanted to be on the radio. I took my recorder and just a few minutes into the interview he called it a day. I wasn't angry - just frustrated and disappointed for him.

Sadly, Bill died much too young in 2007, at the age of just 50.

CHAPTER 63

Chris Cheverton

THE LATE CHRIS CHEVERTON was the first person to appear twice in my IW *Weekly Post* Sports Personality column. I have 16 scrapbooks full of local sports stars who appeared in that column and on the opening page of the very first one is Chris. He was my first ever *Post* Sports Personality on Friday November 28, 1975. He was featured again in August 1987. Six years later he shared my *Ryde Times* Sports Personality feature with another local football legend, Barry Allen.

When I first interviewed him he was playing for Brading Town – and the end of his career was still nowhere in sight. Chris was such an influential player in every team he played for. At that time he was enthusing over local players like Viv Hallett, Barry Allen and John Rayner.

'Chiv', who grew up in Yarmouth, could have made the Football League. As it was, he played top Southern League soccer for Waterlooville, after helping Basingstoke win the then powerful Hampshire League title three times in a row.

He had been spotted by Southampton whilst still a schoolboy and joined them as an amateur. An early highlight for him was the week he spent at Lilleshall, under coach Joe Mercer. Among the other unknowns on that course were George Best, Ralph Coates, John Sissons, Harry Redknapp and John Radford.

At that time he didn't really have support from his family.

"Dad thought professional football was somewhat rocky and he was very doubtful and suggested I went to university. I was dead keen to become a pro footballer but dad was probably right."

He took the advice and studied at Southampton University. Eventually he became a teacher. Locally, he played in one of the finest Newport teams of the post-war years. He almost got a second chance of the pro game and was invited to a trial at the Dell by Ted Bates, who'd seen him play for Newport when they won the Hampshire Senior Cup. Just a couple of days before this was due to happen he went down with a serious illness and was out of football for a year.

Many Islanders, including me, felt he would have made it but for the illness.

Modest as ever, he told me: "I was never the same after my illness – but I suspect I wasn't quite good enough. I lacked pace."

One of his greatest disappointments was when Newport lost to Bristol Old Georgians in the last 32 of the FA Vase. It was a last minute goal and the Island team had fancied their chances of getting to Wembley.

After his days in top non-league football Chris returned to play locally for Newport, East Cowes Vics and Brading. He played well into his 40s and was as enthusiastic and influential as ever. Many young Island youngsters benefitted from his experience. He was always keen to put something back into the game he loved and became the secretary of Newport Football Club.

Chris had chosen his career well. He became an iconic Island teacher and eventually a deputy head.

Former Island cricket skipper Bill Jenkins once told Chris: "Play until you can't play anymore." He did just that. In fact, he was also a super cricketer in a brilliant Newport team. He did captain the team to league and cup honours and played over 20 times for the Island representative team.

When he came on my radio show it was following the Kinks record of A *Dedicated Follower Of Fashion*. He was also the Island's best dressed footballer – and even had stubble long before it became the trend. We miss you Chris.

CHAPTER 64

Adam Hose & Chris Russell

IN MY LAST BOOK I wrote about the joy of interviewing two local cricketers, David Griffiths and Danny Briggs, who went on to play first class cricket. It's been such a remarkable few years and Adam Hose and Chris Russell complete a formidable quartet of home grown talents to have played top class cricket. Adam, who is now with Warwickshire, is rapidly making a name for himself and what a pleasure to sit and watch him bat in televised games. Chris Russell is now back on the Island helping young cricketers at Ventnor, after playing several years for Worcestershire.

Adam Hose

Adam is the son of Jeff Hose, a legendary Island cricketer who was good enough to have played county cricket but he started playing later than his son and did not get the same opportunities. Amazingly, Adam played in a Ventnor men's team at the age of eight and took two wickets for two runs. From around the age of five he went to games with his father and loved the players to bowl a few balls at him in the practice nets.

A few years later, when he was on the Lords ground staff as one of the MCC Young Cricketers, he was 12th man for the full England team. An occasion he will never forget – and he went on to field for a while in a Test Match.

He told me: "Being in the dressing room with some of the world's top cricketers and to watch how they prepare was a very valuable experience. They were just normal guys who were good at what they do."

Adam had matches for the second teams of Hampshire, Glamorgan and Worcestershire but is was Somerset who spotted his potential and gave him his first contract. After some huge scores, including a double hundred for the second XI, he made their one day team and quickly made a name for himself at a county where Viv Richards and Ian Botham had made them world famous. Since our interview he was head hunted by Warwickshire and has played both county and one day cricket for them.

Chris Russell

Chris Russell, who also began his cricket at Ventnor, made national headlines in 2012 when he took six wickets for Worcestershire in a game against South Africa. These included "South Africa Blown Away By Russell" and "England Shown The Way By Russell."

Soon after that he made his County Championship debut against Warwickshire, at Edgbaston, and dismissed Lee Westwood with his second ball. In all, he made 40 appearances for his county first team in various forms of the game. He bowled at an incredible 90mph and among his prize wickets were JP Duminy, Glenn Maxwell, Alviro Petersen and Nick Compton. He also played against Australia, New Zealand and Pakistan.

One of the great disappointments of his professional career was being the country's leading wicket taker in the group stages of the Twenty20 competition and then being dropped.

Chris spent our winters playing in South Africa with England Test player Dawid Malan. In his last season he took 60 wickets for his club side, Belleville CC.

Was being a professional hard work? "My mates told me to get a real job but it was tough. You could get no time off from March to September but I enjoyed it."

When I interviewed Chris it was on the eve of the 2018 season, when he came home to skipper Ventnor. His team got better and better as the season progressed and he was the leading wicket taker in their division of the Southern League. His passion for the game was very evident.

Both these successful cricketers pointed out how people like Sam Garaway and John Hilsum, among others, had been such an influence in their early days at Ventnor.

CHAPTER 65

Bob Humphray

WHEN I INTERVIEWED 88 year old Bob Humphray in 1997 it was to celebrate the 50th anniversary of his Whitecliff Bay Holiday Park. He was delighted to be still working and most days it was 7am to midnight. Before the centre had opened in 1947 Bob had dug the 575 foot sewer single handed. They didn't have that much money – in fact it was just £600 to build the toilet black.

Bob was lucky to be there at all. When he was born in the Fleming Arms at Binstead he was, in his own words, "half dead." He was fed bullocks blood which pulled him through.

Bob had some vivid wartime memories including watching the convicts march from Brading Station to the downs to dig trenches. "Us kids used to watch them and sometimes they brought us bags of sweets. We'd watch them eat their lunch which was always corn beef sandwiches."

He began life as a boat builder at Woodnutt's in Bembridge. When he started to play the drums he found himself working seven days and seven nights a week. The bands he played with appeared at regular dances all around the Island.

When the second world war came along Bob was involved with building torpedo boats and Uffa Fox's brilliantly designed airborne lifeboats. Just after the war he had the idea for the holiday park. In the last year of the war Bob was involved in supplying bands for the local holiday camps. That stuck in his mind and when peace returned he decided, as they had a spare field on the farm, they aught to try it. What an astute observation that was and his brothers were all in agreement. They built two caravans, which were virtually new on the scene, and made 25 chalets from old army service huts that were being sold off. Our Bob was rather clever when he purchased the huts.

"I bought most of them and the other farmers got a bit het-up about it all. Not being boat builders, they didn't realise the bearers under the huts were made of Columbian Pine. They were planed and 20 foot in length. That was worth more than the other lot put together. Nobody else knew and I never told them. I sold them back to the farmers without the bearers."

There were not many cars in those days and people used to arrive by bus. They survived the Polio scare and never looked back. Over the 50 years their holidaymakers rose from 200 a week to 1500.

Bob was clever and he turned the old hay loft into the Culver Club. This became famous all around the Island. They had a few stars visit. I saw Shane Richie, Leslie Crowther, Jack Warner and Ricky Valance. I also interviewed Tom Watt, Lofty from *EastEnders*, when he stayed on site.

The Humphray family always catered for families. Some of the household name holiday centres became adult only, as people were retiring earlier. They also acquired the Whitecliff Bay Hotel that had been owned by the Terry-Wood family, who ran Shanklin Pier. This prompted another memory for Bob.

"These days no-one wants to walk anywhere. They all want to take their cars. When us lads were younger we would walk across the downs from Whitecliff Bay to Shanklin Pier just for a dance. We'd be back on top the downs around 2.30am and get home about half an hour later. Some of my brothers had to be up at 5.30 to milk the cows."

On the day of our interview one lady had told him she'd been coming for 35 years. Cheeky as ever, Bob added: "I told her that deserved a kiss and she liked it."

Now the Whitecliff Bay Holiday Park is owned by a large mainland group. That's progress – or is it?

CHAPTER 66

Alex Dyke

BACK IN THE SUMMER of 1984 I received my first-ever begging letter. Well, it was several, actually. They were all from a young Island DJ who was desperate to appear in my *Weekly Post* Stage Talk column. He knew I was always keen to help local youngsters. I have always admired people who try and try again. He told me how good he was and could I come down to Sandown's Court Jester to see him work. I turned up and had a surprise – he was good. That was the first time I ever met Alex Dyke.

I'd also tuned in to *Radio Solent's Something Else*, their early evening show, from Monday to Friday. Alex was a co-host of a programme you either loved or hated. I was not a regular listener but he did well. At that time, Alex also bombarded radio stations with

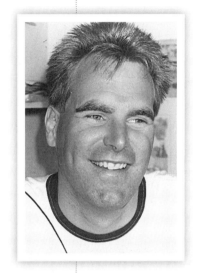

demo tapes – and I guess begging letters. He also knew that *Radio 1's* Gary Davies and *Radio Clyde's* Bill Padley, a fellow Islander, had both gone down that route. As I'm writing this chapter he's back on *Radio Solent*, after a somewhat controversial career, and is proving very popular.

Make no mistake, Alex is a great broadcaster and he should have made national radio but, at times, he's been his own worst enemy. Longing to be an American-style shock jock, like his idol Howard Stern, he sometimes spoke out – and then engaged his brain. It did get him into a few scrapes. Some were deliberate, I'm sure.

During my media career, I've seen two very different sides of Alex Dyke. At times he's been so helpful and arranged interviews for me and gone out of his way to be of service. On one occasion, he just gave me a number of boxed vinyl compilation albums and they have been so useful. I remember when he pleaded with me to have the IW Radio scoop that I had been to Surrey to interview Cliff Richard. I gave in, of course. There were times when he wasn't so kind towards me. I don't hold grudges and we've had some fun on his *Radio Solent* shows since then. He's been happy to plug my books.

Over the years I've heard some brilliant radio shows from him and he's always so full of ideas. He never just goes through the motions. He clearly loves radio – and it shows. He's a definite one-off but has now clearly mellowed with age.

Alex had an audition for *Top Of The Pops* and would have been perfect but they chose some inferior presenters. He has worked in America and on other British local radio stations. He occasionally presents a few items on *South Today*, with his usual enthusiasm and vast knowledge of pop music.

Sadly, one or two of his greatest heroes have fallen from grace in recent years, which has been a great disappointment to him.

Alex has come a long way since he became a Shanklin Youth Club DJ in 1974. He had great self-belief then – and still has.

In his early days he worked at The Beachcomber, Bogey's, Keats Inn, Zanies and Julises. He even had a spell on *Radio Luxembourg*.

I can vividly remember when he appeared on my *Solent* TV show called *Hannam's Half Hour*. This was also seen on Sky Television. I even had a few calls from around the country from people who knew Alex. One person even suggested I gave him a rough time. What me?? I was once described by the CP's controversial former columnist, Charlotte Hofton, as being at the 'soft end of the market'.

The only time I've ever been jealous of an Alex Dyke interview was when Robert Stigwood said yes to him and no to me. Mind you, he might have been envious of one or two of mine.

CHAPTER 67

Andrew Turner

BACK IN THE SUMMER of 2003 on a beautiful June day I was sat on the banks of the River Thames being treated to a Houses of Parliament lunch by the Island's MP and his then partner Carole Dennett. I did think of my late father for a while because I knew he would not have been impressed. With him being a red hot Labour supporter and a strong trade unionist I would have been in trouble for the company I was keeping. Unlike him, I have never been interested in party politics or associated with any particular party. I have always voted for the person who I thought would be the best MP for the Island, if elected. That list had included Steve Ross, Peter Brand, Barry Field and Andrew.

I had never realised until just prior to that interview with our sitting MP that he'd been a school teacher for seven years and specialised in geography. He did have a tough baptism at a Birmingham comprehensive school but survived to enjoy that part of his life.

Westminster was not new to him. After his days as a teacher he did work for the Conservative party and in particular Keith Joseph. He had failed in one or two London elections before moving to the Island to fight the 1997 General Election. He didn't get in – and was not really surprised, as the polls were not in their favour.

Andrew fell in love with the Island and decided to remain here and the local party gave him another chance in the next election – which he won in 2001.

"I did not want to leave the Island and go off and find a safe seat somewhere else. I was happy to stay and fight another contest. I took to the Island people and made the point of not trying to tell them what to do, which was a restraint from my natural instincts," said Andrew. That was a wise decision.

I quickly sensed the passion Andrew had for the job. It was tough with him representing the largest constituency in Britain. The piles of paperwork in his office would have scared some people off. It was not a day to discuss politics. I wanted to see our MP at work and find out more about him as a person.

Over lunch he presented me with his record choices. Instead of the five I needed, it was a list of 20. We managed to prune it down to five. What did he choose? *The Big Country* movie theme, *Red Roses For A Blue Lady*, *The Carnival Is Over*, *Something's Gotten Hold Of My Heart*, sung by Gene Pitney and Marc Almond, and *Little Man You've Had A Busy Day*. The latter was almost a duet. Andrew sang a few bars live and then left the rest to Bing Crosby.

I'd always wanted to know if MPs were friends away from the House of Commons.

"We get on well and don't regard everyone else as an enemy but we treat each other professionally when it comes to where we disagree. You have to cooperate when you have cross party meetings. We have friends from other parties and sometimes dine with them."

During our 30 minute recording a bell rang and suddenly Andrew was up and off. It was a call to vote in the Commons. I quickly paused our chat and later linked it with the Westminster Waltz, which I thought was rather appropriate.

Andrew resigned in 2017. Sadly, he never really had the chance to thank his constituents in the manner he would have wished.

In February of this year we were on the same Red Jet en route to London. He was off to find out all about Brexit and I was off to interview Laura Michelle Kelly. Neither of us would have changed roles.

CHAPTER 68

Brian Sharpe

WHEN I SAW BRIAN SHARPE live on stage in late 2018 at the Pete Hogman Celebration gig at Newport's Strings venue he was just as enthusiasm as when I first saw him back in the 50s, in the Island's most legendary band called the Cherokees. Their story was featured in *The Wight Connections* volume 1.

Brian has been an inspiration to several generations of local musicians. Many are thrilled to just play alongside him. One of his earliest fans was Philip Norman, now one of Britain's foremost rock music writers, who grew up in Ryde. He's penned books on The Beatles, Rolling Stones, Elton John, John Lennon, Paul McCartney and Eric Clapton.

Brian's musical life actually began in a band called Les Paysans. They played their first-ever gig at the Stag Inn, Lake. Brian's own local mentor was the late Martyn Ford and he was in that band along with Robin Young, Crann Davies and Graham White.

It's hard to believe now that he first tried to play music on an old family violin by strumming the makeshift rubber strings

Brian quickly obtained a reputation of being a fine young guitarist and when he joined the already established Cherokees band it was to change his life for ever.

He once told me, during one of our numerous interviews: "They played at the Queens Hall, Newport, on Saturday nights and hundreds turned up. I'd been used to playing to about 15 people. There was no alcohol served in those days and punters had to nip out to a nearby pub."

There certainly was life beyond the Cherokees and when Brian teamed up with another ex-member, their charismatic lead singer Graham Betchley, as Sharpe and Betchley, they went on to play as a local duo for over 20 years. Sadly, the early death of Graham brought an end to their dual life as musicians and close friends.

They both did play in Blue Moon, an Island supergroup of ageless rockers. They once drew an attendance of 2,500 to the Ryde Arena. That was actually the official figure. Those of us who managed to get in knew there must have been over 3000.

Brian could have made the big time but his love for the Island and his wonderful family and friends kept his feet firmly on Island soil.

He played for over 20 years in Hoggie and the Sharpetones, (the late Pete Hogman has a chapter earlier in this book), was a founder of Island folk rock band Smoke and Mirrors and also has played in a local band called Westward.

A few years ago Brian was very ill and thousands of Islanders were willing him to pull through – and he did. It was touch and go for a while. Within a month he was diagnosed with both skin and prostate cancer and then suffered a heart attack and minor stroke.

"When I was going into hospital, following my stroke, I could not even remember my wife's name. As I was about to leave the house I nipped into my music room to make sure I could still play the guitar," said Brian.

Legend is now a word that is too readily banded around. In Brian Sharpe's case, he is most definitely an Island music legend. He is one of the nicest people I have ever met – a real gentleman. My own list of guitar heroes includes Duane Eddy, Scotty Moore, James Burton, Vic Flick, Hank Marvin and 'Sharpy'.

CHAPTER 69

Mike Whitehead

THERE MAY NOT SEEM a natural link between Tommy Steele, the Milky Bar Kid, the *Mary Rose*, the Apollo Theatre, Cliff Richard and *Tales Of The Riverbank*. In fact, there is. They all feature in the life of the Island's Mike Whitehead.

It all really began when his late father, the world famous figurehead carver Jack Whitehead, got him a job at the ATV studios. At first it was merely in the post room – which was not a haunt for some of their major stars. That instantly changed when he became a studio call boy. Then he mingled with the rich and famous. Mike then got promotion to become an assistant floor manager on the station's considerable drama output.

He told me during one of our interviews: "That was scary. The tension was incredible. People in the business didn't last there much after they were 40 because they had nervous breakdowns and other things. The last ten seconds before a live show were the most stressful."

Luckily, he was never seen on screen but a few of his colleagues were not so fortunate. The red light did spell danger. For a while he was in charge of the cut button. If an actor forgot or fluffed his lines, Mike had his thumb ready to press the button which cut all the studio sound, before he shouted the line.

Among his highlights was working with Cliff Richard and Tommy Steele. On one occasion hundreds of girls thought our Mike was Tommy Steele.

"I had a crew cut like Tommy and was told to go out of the stage door, look around and run like hell. The girls all followed and that gave them the chance to sneak him out the back door.

"I also got to know Cliff Richard and the Shadows well, especially Hank Marvin. I also played drums rather badly and was sometimes corrected by Ted Heath drummer Jack Parnell, when I played in our lunch breaks."

Since then, Mike has become a rather accomplished bass player and has been featured on local CDs and at live gigs. I've seen him turn up in village halls to play in the band for musicals or accompany artists. Ironically, his son is now a top professional drummer with West End experience.

Mike joined a small animated film company and ended up working on 26 episodes of *Tales Of The Riverbank*, here on the island. He created all the sound effects, laid the tracks and did all the editing.

"We had quite a time with all the guinea pigs, white rats, hamsters and other animals. We had to try and persuade them to do the things we wanted. If they refused, we had to rewrite the script to what they had actually done."

When Mike was a member of the Plessey Radar Diving Club they were among the early volunteer divers who helped find the *Mary Rose*. On one horrendous occasion he almost drowned. As the standby diver he went in to save a navy diver, without a rope. It was a false signal and the guy was not in danger. Mike certainly was and for a few moments he thought his time was up.

"They managed to pump me out and hide me from my wife until a bit later," revealed Mike.

Sadly, when the wreck became a high powered archaeological dig with millions of pounds available and Prince Charles so heavily involved, some of the local divers left the scene, for varying reasons.

Mike has done some great work for Newport's Apollo Players. I was delighted to choose him for the 2000 *County Press* Amateur Theatre Award for Best Director, for *Blue Remembered Hills*.

Andy Strickland

I'VE ALWAYS LOVED IT when old friends children make a success of their lives. When I played football for Parkhurst Old Boys I occasionally played in their first team alongside far better footballers, like Reggie Strickland. When I received a superb record called *Somewhere On Sea*, by Caretaker Race, I was told by their lead singer, Andy Strickland, that I knew his dad. How right he was.

I also knew Andy's mother, Sheila, through local amateur theatre shows and singing groups. Long before Andy made records with The Loft and Caretaker Race, his mother had made a record live in Ryde Town Hall, at the age of 14. They still had a 78rpm copy of *I Had A Silver Buckle*. There were definitely no plans for a duet.

During his early life on the Island Andy played in a local band called the Confusers, alongside 'Brillo' Brimson, and the Lewis brothers, Mark and Damon. Then he left Ryde High and went to London's Central Poly to undertake a three year course in media studies.

While at college he joined a popular London band called The Loft, who made two singles for MCA. They disbanded in 1985 but four years later Creation Records released a compilation album. In 2006 they reformed for gigs and made a brilliant EP.

Andy also became a freelance pop music writer for the *Record Mirror*. This led him to interviews with world famous star acts like The Smiths, Cure and Talking Heads. Once, in Paris, he was taken out to dinner by Annie Lennox.

In the mid-80s Andy formed his own band, Caretaker Race. I have all their 12 inch vinyl singles and their highly acclaimed album, produced by Stephen Street. He'd produced brilliant tracks by The Smiths. Andy wrote the songs, sang them and played guitar. *Somewhere On Sea* was clearly influenced by the Island.

One day Andy had quite a surprise during an interview with Wedding Present, a Leeds group with over 20 hit records. They told him that is was his guitar solo on the first Loft single that had inspired them to join the music business.

Eventually Caretaker Race decided to disband and it was a sad moment for Andy. They were talented enough to have become a major British group.

"I did have high hopes for the band but we just didn't get the lucky breaks. We parted on a high – a European tour, which was a real ambition achieved," revealed Andy.

With his love of football, doubtless inspired by his dad's love for the game, he went on to work for top soccer magazines like *90 Minutes* and *Goal*. Then he moved to the Football 365 website. Twelve months later he joined www.dotmusic and became their editor At that time they had about 150,000 users per month. Under his guidance it quickly increased to 850,000, worldwide, and then rose to over one million. Andy was in his element and had a staff of over 20.

Andy continues to play music and I was delighted on one occasion to see him in Edana Minghella's backing band. We last met at his Ryde flat in 2014. For some years he also became a DJ at several IW Pop Festivals, where he had his own following.

I've never asked Andy about his football skills but he could never have come close to being in the same class as his late father. Mind you, my old friend Reggie was never known for his singing or guitar talents.

CHAPTER 71

Larry Ellis

I'VE UNDERTAKEN quite a few interviews in Yarmouth. These include Michael Grade, Frankie Vaughan, David Dickinson, Brian Johnston and Phillip Schofield. My partner Bertie, who works in the local pharmacy, tipped me off that a former Fleet Street photographer called Larry Ellis was now living in the town. There was only one problem – I couldn't stop him talking. I wanted 30 minutes and after nearly an hour his patient dog started to bark very loudly. Obviously, he'd had enough.

The Beatles

My head was spinning with fantastic stories of the Beatles, Princess Diana, Roger Moore, the Queen Mother, Brigitte Bardot, the Krays, Sophia Loren, Richard Burton and Clint Eastwood – and they were just a few of the people he'd photographed.

For many years Larry had worked for the *Daily Express* and for some while he also worked for United Artists, who were involved with movies. He visited the sets of Bond movies and Clint Eastwood westerns.

Not many photographers can claim to have had Clint Eastwood

Charlie Chaplin and Sophia Loren

knock on their door to borrow a cup of sugar or have Roger Moore restage a movie car stunt in France, just for him to get his photo. Brigitte Bardot, who he described as "an incredible lady", once bought him a pair of cowboy boots. Those were in the days when the stars liked photographers – and long before the paparazzi came along to haunt them.

Larry had a great scoop when he was the only Fleet Street photographer outside of Princess Diana's Chelsea flat. Her mini wouldn't start, so Larry, with the help of a nearby ITN television crew, gave her a push to start the car.

Richard Burton and Elizabeth Taylor

When the Beatles came on the scene Larry knew a guy who went to work for Brian Epstein. This led him to trips with them to Paris and Stockholm. In the latter city they had five suites booked in a top hotel. The Fab Four had one each and Larry had the other. In London he once knocked on Ringo Starr's door at 1am for a picture. He got it but not until he was forced to watch a film on submarines.

At a Kent college the Queen Mother took pity on Larry. The local police chief did not like photographers and she noticed a couple of

Cary Grant with his daughter

coppers stood right in front of Larry, as she walked by. A little later one of her private detectives invited Larry to get an exclusive photo. He was working for all the Fleet Street papers.

One picture that Larry locked away and never used was when he followed a North Finchley MP around for a week to cover a story on her. She was not well known at the time – and her name was Margaret Thatcher. On the hustings he took a picture of her climbing on to a Land Rover and it revealed her stocking tops.

What a life he's had! This page includes some of his great photos of the Beatles, Sophia Loren and Charles Chaplin, Taylor and Burton and Cary Grant with his own daughter.

CHAPTER 72

Roger Mazillius

OVER THE PAST 40 YEARS I have interviewed many performers who were discovered at London's famous 2 I's coffee bar. These have included Cliff Richard, Jet Harris, Hank Marvin, Bruce Welch, Tommy Steele, Wee Willie Harris and Adam Faith. I did interview another guy who had performed there but he didn't become a star. Instead, he became an Island publican, shop owner and councillor. I still find it hard to believe it was Roger Mazillius.

Back in 1957 Roger was part of a group who won the all-Middlesex skiffle competition and famous skiffler Johnny Duncan was one of the judges. They beat a group called the Worried Men and won £25 and four live gigs.

Roger revealed the story in my feature on him in the Island Life magazine.

"One day I was walking past the 2 I's and noticed the Worried Men were going to be appearing there. I went inside and told the manager that our group had beaten them in the Middlesex contest and we should be booked to appear there. It worked - and we played in the interval two nights later."

There was not a happy ending. The 2 I's Worried Men was not the same group that Roger's band had beaten. In their line-up were Wee Willie Harris and Terry Nelhams, who later became Adam Faith. Mr Nelhams was not too happy another group were using their name.

In 1970 Roger moved to the Island with his super wife Jill and continued to study law for a couple of years. Then they took over the Wishing Well pub at Pondwell. There he encouraged local bands and musicians. He did make one error of judgement.

"I actually turned down the genus of Level 42, who included Mark King and the Gould brothers, in favour of another local band called Shimera, who were brilliant and played the music of Crosby, Stills and Nash. As it happened, that other band became Level 42. That must question my musical preferences."

During Roger's residency at the Wishing Well the venue became a hotbed for top quality darts. He became chairman of the IW County Darts and helped take local players to new heights. He also featured world class players in Sunday night exhibition games. These included John Lowe, Alan Evans and Leighton Rees.

Somehow, Roger got talked into running the St Helens Road Race. He hadn't run for several years. When 69 year old Bill Ross passed him that was the spur he needed to really get fit.

When the first Island Athletic Championships were held at Smallbrook, Roger won six medals – and a bet with his good mate Nobby Nash. A local charity profited from this.

Later he managed the new Westridge Centre and then opened Vectis Model Auctions in Cowes. They created a record by selling a rare Dinky Toy Foden truck for £6000.

Roger first became a local councillor for Seaview and Nettlestone in the late 70s but business commitments curtailed his time and he eventually gave up. Later he made a comeback and won a seat at Northwood. A year or two later he became the chairman of the IW Council and was very honoured to be selected.

I think Roger would have loved to have been a pop star. Forty years after that 2 I's gig he wrote a song called A *Girl Named Sue*. I even played it on *John Hannam Meets*. It had a modern lyric and would have been banned in the days of skiffle.

I had to ask him one final question? Was he the notorious Mole Man in the IW *Weekly Post*? All I got was a broad smile but I'm sure there was a giveaway glint in his eye.

CHAPTER 73

Lucy Baker

AS A FAMILY we went to a pantomime at Sandown Pavilion in the early 80s and on the way home we all had to choose our favourite person in it. Surprisingly, none of us chose one of the principals. We were all most impressed with a very young dancer who was in the Hilary Hall Dancers. Her name was Lucy Baker and I found out her father was Gus Baker, a good friend, who was a Sandown school teacher and played rugby for the Hurricanes.

A year or two later I did a feature on her in my *Weekly Post* Stage Talk column. At the time she was ten and the second to smallest person at her school. She'd already played Molly in *Annie*, for the South Wight Youth Theatre, and scored 91 per cent for both drama and recorder in Island music festivals. Amazingly, she had also passed an audition for the famous Arts Educational School at Tring. Their past pupils had included Julie Andrews, Evelyn Laye and David Hemmings.

She told me at the time: "I would really like to be an entertainer like Bonnie Langford. She is very musical. I don't want to go on to be another Liberace – or is he a painter?"

Sadly, the IW Council decided she was too young to have a grant. Her parents did agree with this. Ironically, if it had been for the Royal Ballet, that would have been different.

One evening in 1986 I had an exciting phone call from Gus. Lucy was then 11 and had been chosen to appear in *Jane Eyre*, as Adele, with two major stars, Keith Michell and Jenny Seagrove, for a summer season at the famous Chichester Festival Theatre. Thanks to her dad, I had another Stage Talk scoop.

During that summer she was allowed to appear in 34 performances and was on stage for 90 minutes. There has always been strict guidelines for young children of school age.

After the run she told me: "It's been such a great experience and like a dream come true. You do work hard though, with long rehearsals."

Up until then, it had been Chichester's most successful production ever.

What of Keith Michell? "He was very nice to me but very demanding."

Lucy and Jenny Seagrove, the huge star from *Woman Of Substance*, became such good friends and Jenny was surprised to find out there was a Seagrove Bay on the Island, near to where Lucy lived. Gus and his wife Marie used to send her pictures of it – and even named their cat after her.

This friendship between Jenny and Lucy has continued throughout the years.

The last time I interviewed Jenny was in late 2017 at London's Phoenix Theatre, when she was appearing in *The Excorcist*. We talked about her long friendship with Lucy. It's a small world. My daughter, Caroline, was the Head of Wardrobe on that show.

Four years after Lucy's Chichester *Jane Eyre* season she was invited back to join the cast of *The Silver King*, alongside Tony Britton, Alan Howard and Brian Glover.

"I was lucky they still remembered me and were able to find me again. The auditions meant I had to miss a day from school – and a maths lesson, so I was particularly pleased."

After a few years Lucy decided not to head for a career in showbusiness but she has such wonderful memories to look back on.

CHAPTER 74

Roger French

ROGER FRENCH HAS ALWAYS BEEN one of those guys who's genuinely pleased to see you. Which is just as well, because he was a former heavyweight boxing champion and won 14 of his 54 fights inside the distance – and he only lost three times. Back in 1987 hundreds of Islanders were also so pleased to see Roger. His fencing company worked 17 hours a day, after the hurricane had left a trail of broken wood.

Over the years Roger has been generous in sponsoring so many local sporting events. He's always had the desire to help local youngsters.

Many had high hopes for Roger in the boxing world. As a schoolboy fighter he weighed in at 14 stone 2 pounds. Twice he won the Southern Counties title. He also boxed for the Newport Amateur Boxing Club.

Back in 1993 he told me: "Boxing was so popular when I was a youngster. Tickets for our contests at the Newport Drill Hall sold out two months before the event. As a schoolboy I was so keen and trained really hard. I did a six-o'clock paper round and then went for a run."

British boxing star Freddie Mills got to hear about young Roger.

"He wanted me to give up working at Morey's and turn professional, at his training camp. Perhaps I should have gone through with it. He told me to get cauliflower ears and a flat nose and I'd be perfect. I wasn't too keen on that."

Roger took up squash rather late in his life but quickly progressed through the ranks, from division 19, to rival people like Dave Horne and Gribble Smith. Once on a visit to the West Indies he got to the quarter finals of their open event.

In the early 70s Roger left Morey's to start his own firm. It corresponded with the Dutch Elm Disease and meant he was very busy. Never being afraid of hard work Roger was in his element.

"Because people trusted us I got a lot of insurance work following the hurricane. We got wood direct from local forests. Although I was the boss I liked being on site with the lads. It was all about personal service and I loved to put the finishing touches to the jobs."

By 1993 Roger was encouraged to slow down. His hard work, particularly after the hurricane, played havoc with his heart. His pulse rate dropped to 34 but no-one locally could find out what was wrong with him. Eventually Roger and his wife Jean, who now writes great children's books, decided to emigrate to Spain. Being a self-confessed workaholic he just had to get away and the longer he stayed here he would not take it easy.

"It wasn't until I got to Spain that my heart problems were really sorted out. I saw one of the top two surgeons in the country and was treated that same afternoon. They told me with a pulse rate of 29, I was clinically dead. They did a fantastic job and fitted a pacemaker. It gave me a new lease of life."

Despite his great love of Spain, Roger decided to come back to the Island in 2011 and they now have a flat on the banks of the River Medina. Even before he moved back here he told me, on a visit home: "I could never sever my ties with the Island. My roots are here."

He still keeps fit and I often see him working outside of his son's home in Rookley. Either sorting out a fence or sweeping up the grass and leaves.

I was going to challenge him to an over 60s boxing match, for guys with pacemakers. Then thought better of it. I'm not a vain person but I don't fancy cauliflower ears or a flat nose – and he's younger than me.

CHAPTER 75

Sarah Scotcher

SOME PEOPLE ARE BORN to be professional entertainers, others are lucky to have even got a break and there are those who should have made it but it just never happened. I think Shorwell's Sara Scotcher falls into the last category. I've seen her steal a pantomime by simply walking on stage. Audiences love the expectation of what to expect next – and you can bet it's a laugh. In more recent years her directing talents have limited her own stage opportunities.

I first saw her back in 1988 when she was part of a clever magical act called Zira, with Simon Leigh. She was then Sarah Jane Daniels. They were at a Whitegold Showcase for hotel and holiday centre bookers. Her dream was for a professional career in musical comedy and, via magic, she hoped to obtain her Equity card. They worked all along the south coast and at a top London cabaret club. Sometimes they practised 12 hours a day to produce their stylish act.

Initially, she'd worked here for Lloyds TSB, at Newport and Freshwater. There were no computers in those days to make things easier. It was always considered to be a kind of special job.

Nowadays it's hard to believe that as a schoolgirl she was bullied and lacked any real confidence. A change of school did help but a lady called Nesta Meech, so well known in Island amateur theatre circles, was just the inspiration she needed. Joining her dance classes changed her life for ever.

"I really owe it all to Nesta. She boosted my confidence and I appeared in all of her shows and eventually thought about a professional career in showbusiness," said Sarah, back in 2013.

During her teens Sarah appeared in plays for the Shorwell Drama Group and continued to dance for Nesta Meech. This led to three seasons in professional summer shows at Ryde Pavilion, as one of the 4 Valentines dance troupe. They worked alongside experienced acts like Billy Whittaker and Mimi Law, Des King, and Mitchell Armstrong.

When Zira finally disbanded she formed a song and dance double act with the Island's Mandy Hutchings. They became Pure Chance and performed at local hotels. By this time Sarah had met and married Tony Scotcher and led a double for a while, as a mother and cabaret performer. The girls gave up when hotels wanted musicians to play the whole evening.

Sarah realised she would not obtain her dream but continued to entertain via the Wight Strollers. If she had been born a few years later, it could have been so different. Laura Michelle Kelly proved that – and others have followed in her wake.

"I still go to a lot of shows and you can never stop learning. The minute you start thinking you know it all, it starts closing down and your performances and productions suffer."

Since I last interviewed her, Sarah has achieved one theatre dream. She has directed a musical. This was *Priscilla* at Newport's Medina Theatre.

Most of her time is now spent directing. This can be fun but also quite frustrating at times. Especially in her Shorwell pantomimes when one of their stalwarts has forgotten his lines and makes up his own script. You've already read about Ian Dockray.

Entertaining is now a Scotcher family tradition. I have seen her daughter, Emily, play some outstanding roles and Ed, her son, has followed suit. I have also seen her husband as the rear end of a camel and as one of 'The Stars' of Shorwell pantos. The backstage boys always take centre stage for one routine and bring the house down.

CHAPTER 76

Tony Grimwade

I'VE ALWAYS LOVED CHATTING to Tony Grimwade and could listen to his football stories for hours. The first time I met him – well actually it was really the first time I saw him – I couldn't get close enough to meet him. I was playing in defence for East Cowes Vics Reserves against St Helens. We had some promising young players, including Cliff Light and Robbie Mitchell. We all had spells of trying to mark him but I guess, unsuccessfully. He scored ten and we lost 14-1.

The last time I met him for an interview, he was up a ladder at his old pink house in Seaview. He soon came down to reminisce about the old days. I did skip the 14-1 story. I interviewed him for newspapers, magazines and radio. Such a modest guy who just had the knack of being in the right place at the right time. Some games he was anonymous for about 80 minutes and then popped up from nowhere to score twice in the last ten minutes.

"All I could do was put the ball in the net," said Tony, back in 1987. They pay millions today for someone who can do that.

How good was he? Well he scored well over 1000 goals during his career. At the age of 37 he even turned down the chance to play Southern League soccer for Dorchester. They offered him £30 a week, which was a lot of money in those days. Years later Gosport offered local football stars Steve Greening and Gareth Williams a £500 signing on fee to play for them in the Southern League – and they took it. In 1976, while playing for Newport, he scored against Southampton's FA Cup winning side, who played a friendly at Church Litten. They including Peter Osgood and co and won 4-1 – and brought the FA Cup over with them.

During his illustrious 25 year career Tony, affectionately known as Gribble, played for St Helens, Ryde Sports, Seaview, Brading, Newport and East Cowes Vics. Just occasionally, since his retirement, Tony gets down the old scrap books and, amazingly can remember every goal and how he scored them. Well, he could back in '87. I bet he still can.

In 1984 I tempted him out of retirement to play for the John Hannam Sports Personality XI against the TV Entertainers at Westridge. The Coronation Street lads feared no better than Island defences.

"I was shattered after about 20 minutes but three goals came along," said Tony. I think we won 6-1 and Nigel Pivaro, Michael Le Vell, Sean Wilson and Phil Daniels were not too happy.

Tony's last competitive game, prior to the Corrie charity match, was in 1982. St Helens, his first and last club, won the Hampshire Junior A Cup with a 2-0 win over the very strong Soldiers Return team. He got them both. A few years before then, Seaview won the Hampshire Intermediate Cup by beating the highly fancied RTC Aldershot army team. The score was 4-1 and he got all four.

Another magical memory was when Island League Brading beat Hampshire League professionals Newport, the Island's top team, in the IW Gold Cup. It was 2-1 and A Grimwade got one of them.

Tony could not attend a trial game at Portsmouth because of injury. Pompey never got back to him and eventually signed Ray Hiron from Fareham – but he wasn't as good as Tony.

Some managers expected him to run all over the field. That just wasn't his game. Rumours suggest he only ever scored two goals from outside of the penalty area.

How's this for a tongue twister. When Tony was a boat builder at Woodnutt's, St Helens, they displayed a banner which read: "Woodnutt's Gribble Guts Grimwade Goal Grabber From Goose."

CHAPTER 77

Phyllida Crowley-Smith

BACK IN 1977 Wootton's Phyllida Crowley-Smith was seen briefly on stage at Newport's Apollo Theatre, as a little girl in the park, in the musical *Salad Days*. Just over 20 years later she was playing in London's biggest West End hit, *Phantom Of The Opera*.

Philly's mother, Miriam, taught my children at Godshill Primary and also ran her own dancing school. So it wasn't really a surprise that her daughter would end up a dancer. Well, actually, it was a little tricky early on. At the age of six she threatened to leave mum's class and give it all up. How lucky she was to be talked out of it. Perhaps it was all due to the pink tutu she wore on her first appearance at the IW Musical Festival.

"I was quite large at the time and it was all totally new to me." She went on to become one of the most successful pupils ever at this annual event.

After that brief appearance in *Salad Days*, Philly made her speaking debut in the Apollo's The Provoked Wife. Then she danced in the Sandown Operatic Society's musical *Oklahoma*.

At Medina High she appeared in *Grease* and a mini version of *Hamlet*. During her training at the Bush Davies College in Sussex she won their Dancer of the Year title and the Noreen Bush Award for classical ballet.

Her professional debut was at Wimbledon Theatre in their 1987 pantomime *Robinson Crusoe*. What a cast, too! Dennis Waterman, Rula Lenska, Colin Baker and Jan Leeming. Soon afterwards she toured Britain in *Oklahoma*, which starred my good friend Tony Adams. Millions of ladies loved him as Doctor Bywaters in *General Hospital* and Adam Chance in *Crossroads*.

I used to love it when Miriam would ring me to say her daughter was on her way home for a few days and would I like to pop down to Wootton to have a chat. I wrote about her in the *Weekly Post* and had her several times as a live guest on my radio show.

On one occasion I did a feature on Philly in the *County Press*. Before I'd even had time to buy a paper I had an early morning phone call from her mother. She told me she loved the article but who was the girl in the photograph? I remember her saying: "John, it's not Phyllida. Who is it?" I have never found out. It was in my photo file with Philly's name on the back. By the way, I have checked the photograph on this page.

I remember going up to Her Majesty's Theatre, London, to see her on stage in *Phantom*. I felt very proud when she brought the house down with her solo dance. No pink tutu on that occasion. Philly also played the White Rabbit in the hit DVD version of *Cats*. John Mills was in that one. Another of her great triumphs was appearing in Cliff Richard's *Heathcliff*. Her husband, Jimmy Johnston, was one of the leading actors in that West End show. One night Cliff took them out to dinner after the show. Her other productions include *Chitty Chitty Bang Bang* and *Mary Poppins*.

In more recent years Philly has also choreographed numerous shows. Her movie credits include the super movie *Beyond The Sea*, which was the Bobby Darin story.

Now Philly is passing on her skills and experience to budding young dancers. She is the head of dance at Guildford School of Acting.

CHAPTER 78

Reuben Abbott

I NEVER TIRE of going up to Staplers Farm, Newport, once more commonly known as the Lavender Farm. Now it's more associated with roses and antiques. It's home to one of the Island's great characters, Reuben Abbott. Some say he's a Dick Strawbridge look-a-like. I'd never heard of him! After Reuben told me this, I went straight home and watched one of Dick's television programmes – and it was hard to spot the difference.

Long before I knew Reuben I was aware of his superb skills at relaying a hedge. Him and his brother, Paul, had worked wonders on a long hedge on the road from the Godshill Dogs Home into the village. It was just exciting to see the progress they made – and they never took a tea break every ten minutes.

Another fan of the Lavender Farm was the late Geoffrey Hughes. I first met him there for an interview for IW Radio. He chose the Abbott's lounge to pre-record the interview. In fact, the family have been at the farm for over 90 years. This may surprise a few – but Reuben hasn't been there quite that long. Apparently, he's younger than he looks! His great grandfather was there in 1927.

"I've been blessed with a really good family and I had such a great childhood. I was driving the tractor as a ten year old and could milk the cows when I was quite young. I started hedge laying and hurdle making when I was 12."

He loved taking up the cold tea and tomato sandwiches in a red leather bag up to his grandfather, who was driving the tractor. In a cold winter, he and other youngsters would skate on the farm's frozen pond and jump over an old tree and stay upright.

During his life Reuben has been the Island's champion ploughman on five occasions. He's one of only three men, in over 100 years, to win the title in three consecutive years. Was there a secret to his successes?

"The knack is you have to be as stubborn as you can be. It's a battle between you and the soil. Don't worry about the other people in the competition. Just keep an eye on the soil, which can change very quickly."

When Reuben started ploughing there were no air-cooled tractor cabs, with music and all mod cons. It would have been heaven for him to listen to Matt Monro through the speaker system. He had to sit on an old wartime tractor, which was open to all the elements.

Staplers was primarily a dairy farm but they did have pigs. According to him, they loved their bellies being scratched. Rumours suggest he does, too.

They also had quite a name for showing poultry. It was no surprise for him to see chickens being bathed in the kitchen sink. They were lathered all over and had olive oil rubbed on their legs. No, I didn't ask him the obvious. He wouldn't fit into the sink anyway!

Reuben will willingly talk about most things but he remains fiercely tight-lipped about one subject. He was one of a select band of guys who were invited to regular 'boys only' nights at Compton Farm, by the legendary Den Phillips. Den would never tell me and neither will Reuben. I know it wasn't all just cakes and buns.

I was allowed a real scoop at Staplers Farm. On one visit I was given a 1962 tape of an Island Archers-type radio soap, performed by local characters. They even allowed me to play it on my radio show. Reuben was probably not even born when that was recorded. Dick Strawbridge was only three.

CHAPTER 79

Richard Wright

WHENEVER I MEET Island journalist Richard Wright I worry if he doesn't insult me. His sarcastic jibes have always kept me very amused. One Sunday morning a few months ago I was running from Island Harbour to Newport and back when I saw Richard and his young partner walking towards me. I slowed down in anticipation – and was not disappointed. His comment was: "Good God! You're still alive then."

Back in 1983 young Richard had been asked by the *Portsmouth News* to interview Cilla Black, during her summer season at Sandown Pavilion. At that time I was writing my Stage Talk column in the *Weekly Post*, which was also owned by the *News*. He didn't want to do it. I guess it wouldn't have been good for his street cred to interview Miss Black. Yes, even he was trendy at one time – especially during a hot summer when he wore his linen suit and John Lennon glasses. I volunteered to undertake the blind date with Cilla – and was made most welcome.

It took nearly 25 years to invite him on to my radio show. He still insists he invited himself. I recorded it on location at the *County Press* offices. We were both rather privileged – it was recorded in the boardroom. He'd rarely been that high in the building before then. He loved choosing his music and actually began with the first record he'd ever bought – and he still had it.

"It was Come Together by the Beatles and I bought it in Teagues record shop. I only got it because I loved the bass line – and still do. I can't stand Paul McCartney but the bass on that is absolutely fantastic."

When Richard first joined the *County Press* they still had adverts on the front page. They had very little sport, two broadsheet pages of every Island court case and an obvious political leaning.

"I used to cover all the court cases and they included everything. I even found out that our sports editor, Alan Harvey, had been a real criminal by not getting his library books back on time."

I used to see Richard freezing in the East Cowes Vics football stand on a cold winter afternoon, when the east wind blew into our faces. I had the feeling he just didn't want to be there.

"In those days we could earn a little extra money by phoning half-time reports to the *Southampton Sports Echo* and the *Portsmouth Football Mail*. We had to run down the road to the public phone box to phone our copy over and hope nobody was in there."

When Richard was working for the IW News Agency he got the first tip off that three prisoners had escaped from Parkhurst Prison. They got a taxi and were hoping to steal a plane from a local airport. It was the busiest night of his life and his stories appeared on the front pages of all the national newspapers and he was interviewed by numerous other media outlets.

When he finally retired from the *County Press* his army of gardening fans missed his regular column. He took up his computer again and made a comeback. They even updated his photograph.

The Duke of Edinburgh was not a Richard Wright fan. Prince Philip once said to him, at an Island function: "You are a very impertinent young man." Richard had made a reference to something the Duke had recently done – in jest, of course. Apparently, the *Weekly Post* photographer took a picture of the Duke eyeballing Richard with a look of real hatred. Luckily, he wasn't locked up in Carisbrooke Castle, although at one time he'd looked like Charles I.

CHAPTER 80

Martin Woodward

I THINK I FIRST TOOK AN INTEREST in diving back in the 50s when the 'Buster' Crabb story made world headlines. My interest was rekindled in the summer of 2018, when I saw the brilliant production of SS *Mendi*, *Dancing The Death Drill*, at the Nuffield City Centre Theatre in Southampton. This was the story of the ship that sank several miles south of the Island, in January 1917, with the loss of 646 lives. When I found out the wreck had been discovered by our own Martin Woodward, I just had to find out more.

We'd last met when he came live into my radio show in 1993. A visit to his fantastic shipwreck museum in Arreton Barns quickly led to another interview. Within a few

days he was appearing on the same *John Hannam Meets* as one of my favourite actors, Jack Ellis. He's probably best known for playing prison officer Jim Fenner in *Bad Girls* and bookmaker Harry Mason in *Coronation Street*. Jack was the star name in the SS *Mendi* production, which featured him and the amazing Isango Ensemble from Cape Town. All those lost in the original tragedy were black South African volunteers en route to join the British Army bound for the Western Front.

Martin, the Island's most famous diver, discovered the wreck in 1974, virtually by accident. At that time he was diving on other known wrecks in the area.

"The strange thing was, I'd never heard of the *Mendi*. I was researching other wrecks but the *Mendi* had never flagged up. It had been a hidden wreck for whatever reason. It may have been kept quiet for propaganda reasons. Perhaps they didn't want people to know about such a large loss of life. That could have been useful propaganda for the Germans and the sad fact it had black troops on board may have had a bearing on it as well, as tragic as that is.

"It was a total surprise. What I expected to find on that particular position, from a vague Admiralty report, was an old lighter dumb barge. I found the unexpected wreck in about 140 metres of water. I realised it was a good quality passenger ship with lots of really good fittings. It really mystified me and on future dives I found a saucer with a shipping company crest of B & A SNC. When I got home I researched it and found it was the British and African Steam Navigation Company. After more research I found it must be the *Mendi*," said Martin.

He's been diving for over 50 years and this proved to be one of his greatest discoveries ever. Initially, he decided not to tell anyone. He did remove a few mementos to act as a memorial to those who were lost.

"I didn't want to keep going back to dive there and bring things up. To me it was really a war grave. I just wanted to leave it in peace. In the following years other divers found out where it was and started to take things off. "

Martin had tried very hard to buy the wreck, so that he could protect it, but there were difficulties about the ownership. He'd never seen the ship's bell but later a diver did bring it up but did not register it. He kept it for about 30 years and then decided he might still get into trouble. He anonymously phoned BBC TV South reporter Steve Humphrey, who was so fascinated by the story, to say it would be left on Swanage Pier on a certain day at 7am – and it was.

Let's hope one day it might come to Martin's museum to put with his few other mementos to honour those 646 who died a few miles south of the Island.

CHAPTER 81

Roy & Ena Hannam

FOR AROUND 30 YEARS East Cowes couple Roy and Ena Hannam were a regular sight for Island motorists. Hundreds of them tooted each time they passed this intrepid couple. They began cycling together in 1930 and, other than a break to have a family, were still peddling into the 1980s. Their total aggregate mileage was not far off 400,000 lifetime miles. Roy's was an incredible 260,000 – and not a crash helmet in sight.

If you ever wondered what ex-racing cyclists did when they became old age pensioners, the answer is simple. They just kept on riding. Roy had been on a cycle ride to Wootton on the day he died and Ena even walked with her faithful bike around the East Cowes shops, to keep her balance. During her final years she reminisced about her cycling trips to fellow residents of Osborne Cottage.

There was such a lot to look back on. They cycled to North Wales on three occasions and twice ventured to Scotland. In 1969 they covered 629 miles around the East Coast. Lands End was another milestone. Their amazing trips were all filmed on home movies and they took these to numerous local WI's, Townswomen's Guilds and local church groups. Roy also added his own sound commentary.

In 1930 Roy became a founder member of the Vectis Roads Cycling Club. Later that year Ena realised, if she wanted to see more of him, she would have to buy her own bike.

On one occasion she told me:" If we saw three cars during a whole evening's cycling it was a lot. Sometimes 120 of us were riding in pairs. On our wedding day we even walked through an archway of cycle wheels."

Roy and Ena were also involved in road and grass track racing. Ena's greatest achievement was coming second in the Alvington Hill Climb. Several guys were embarrassed when she passed them on her way to the top. Roy also once came first in a 50 mile handicap. He was also the secretary of the Vectis Roads for nearly six years.

They started their mainland tours just before the outbreak of war and went to Devon and Cornwall and the Thames Valley. In 1945, with one toddler at home and another on the way, they gave up cycling and sold their bikes.

In the early 50s Roy suffered from a heart attack and coupled with bronchitis and asthma was in a pretty bad state. Dr Dockray, a specialist at Ryde Hospital, then gave him some inspirational advice. Roy took up the story.

"After my illness, Dr Dockray told me to take up golf or cycling. This was a better tonic than any medicine. In 1955 I took to the road again."

Roy and Ena began with short trips around Whippingham but six years later, after regular Island jaunts, went to Devon and Somerset on a 345 mile round trip. Somehow they managed to fit in all their requirements into saddle bags.

Roy and cycling seemed inseparable. In 1977 he lost the sight of one eye and two years later he survived the critical list at St Mary's Hospital, after a severe pulmonary embolism. The will to get back to cycling pulled him through.

Ena once told me, when they appeared in my IW *Weekly Post* Sports Personality column: "In all my cycling days the greatest thrill was seeing Edinburgh in the distance after pedalling from East Cowes. It was out of this world."

Is it just a coincidence that they have the same surname as me? In fact, they were my parents, who were both a great inspiration for me.

CHAPTER 82

Vivien Russell

IN 1978 IF THE SUMMER SHOW producer John Redgrave had stuck with his original plan, Vivien Russell would probably never have arrived on the Island. Right at the last moment he decided to send her to Sandown Pavilion and not Eastbourne. Following that summer with stars like Mike and Bernie Winters, Arthur Worsley and John Boulter, Viv has never gone away.

Falling in love with the Island meant she became a regular in the professional shows at both Sandown Pavilion and Shanklin Theatre. When she was chosen to play alongside Jack Douglas in *Me And My Girl*, at both theatres, she was quite thrilled to be in the same show as the legendary star of stage, television and movies. She could never have imagined they would team up and become partners both on and off stage. Viv gave him great love and support and was such a comfort to him during the last few months of his life.

Viv has been such a great all round entertainer. In her early days she was called a soubrette. A quaint old term for a song and dance act. In her case, it also meant appearing in comedy sketches and anything else that was required in those marvellous seaside concert parties.

When she was growing up, her parents were great radio fans and they loved listening to some of our legendary comics and records by the top American stars of the day. Viv went on to work in summer seasons with comedians like Tommy Trinder and Joe Church and did a memorable Stockton pantomime season with world famous crooner Guy Mitchell.

She appeared in a television show called *Send In The Clowns* and went on to appear in numerous musicals, farces and even a circus. I became such an admirer of her work and saw her give some outstanding performances. There seemed to be nothing she couldn't do. When she came on my television chat show in 1990, she revealed she would love to be in a soap. They missed out. She could have been such an asset to any of them.

Jack Douglas and Viv were such a delightful couple – and he realised how lucky he was. They were also very caring. The first New Year's Eve after Heather died, they were so good to me. With my two young people living on the mainland and my local relatives always tucked up in bed, probably about two hours before the chimes of Big Ben, they didn't want me to be alone that night. So they took me to the Crab Inn at Shanklin.

Viv has always been prepared to put something back into a business she has loved. Her work with the First Act Theatre Company, for adults with learning difficulties, has been outstanding. She has written so many of their pantomimes and narrated them, so they could act along with her. Real emotional moments to savour. Both her and the group's founder, Carol Laidler, have inspired the lives of so many of their clients.

It really had all begun for young Viv when she performed in a dance troupe at the Theatre Royal, Windsor, where they had so many top professional pantomimes. Those enjoyable shows led her to a career in showbusiness. Initially, she wanted to be a ballet dancer but confessed she was the wrong shape. In reality, it was probably much more fun working with stars like Ronnie Hilton, Jan Hunt, Tony Adams, Tom O'Connor – and, of course, Jack Douglas and Guy Mitchell.

In more recent years Viv has been a very active member of the wonderful Friends of Shanklin Theatre. I was thrilled on one of their open nights to be interviewed live on stage by her. It was a kind of Vivien Russell Meets.

CHAPTER 83

Wes Maughan

WHEN I FIRST ARRIVED at Cowes Secondary Modern my sporting heroes were quickly established. They were Peter Butler, who was featured in my third book, and Wes Maughan. Luckily, I've been friends with both for many years. For Wes' story I'm going back to the night of April 8, 1958, at Old Trafford Manchester.

It was the semi-final of the FA Youth Cup. Over the years, the Man United babes had played 43 games in this competition and had never lost. In the first leg at the Dell, against Saints Youth, who were the giantkillers after beating Pompey and Spurs, they had won 5-2 in front of 19, 320. Young Wes Maughan from Cowes scored one of the goals. In the second leg the young Saints won 3-2 in front of a partisan Old Trafford crowd of 17,000, with young Wes scoring twice. In the Reds team were Mark Pearson, Kenny Morgans, Alex Dawson and David Maskell, who all went on to football fame under Matt Busby.

The Saints forward line was Terry Paine, Terry Simpson, Wes Maughan, Peter Vine and John Sydenham, who all went on to play for the Southampton first team, then in the Third Division. In their 6-0 win over Spurs Wes got a hat trick and won praise from Spurs boss Bill Nicholson.

Wes told me." Ted Bates came over to watch the Southampton Football Association youngsters play the Island. We beat them 6-1 and I managed to score four goals. Ted asked Cowes Football Club secretary, Reg Reynolds, if I could play for the Saints Youth team and they agreed."

In his debut season for J S Whites Youth, Wes had scored over 100 goals, After his success for Saints Youth he was offered professional terms by Ted Bates. He initially signed as a semi-pro until he was 21, so he could finish his apprenticeship at J S Whites. Chelsea had also been interested.

At the Dell the Saints had a brilliant forward line of Paine, O'Brien, Reeves, Mulgrew and Sydenham. This made it hard for Wes to get into the team. He did make seven first team appearances. In 101 games for the reserve team he scored 47 goals. Eventually he was sold to Reading and made their first team until an injury finally ended his full-time career.

Shrewdly, he'd qualified as an accountant before going into football. He could play non-league football and still maintain a high power job. So he had two wage packets coming in and was better off than Football League players. His clubs included Chelmsford, Cambridge United and Bexley.

In 1969 he joined American business giants Du Pont. He moved into their emerging computer department and went all around the world. It was a far cry from living at the back of his parent's grocery shop in Cowes.

Wes Maughan was almost too nice to be a pro footballer. His cosy Island family life, idyllic school days and his love for the Salvation Army, he actually played in their band, meant he was far less aggressive than many of his opponents. Wes has always been such a perfect gent – and so nice to know. He made such a wise decision to complete his accountancy qualifications.

Does he envy today's Premiership players? "Not at all. Life's been good to me in everything I've done. I dreamed of becoming a professional footballer and became one. I also had the opportunity to do well in the business world."

He finally got married in 1997 and inherited three boys – all Spurs supporters. They know the story of his hat trick against Spurs Youth off by heart.

I was thrilled a few years ago to be asked by Wes to talk to his Salvation Army group in Staines. We were both a long way from Cowes Secondary.

CHAPTER 84

Tom Clifton

WHEN TOM CLIFTON was a youngster, his father, Paul, who I used to race against in my days as a teenage miler, took him to Heathrow to watch the planes. Young Tom certainly dreamed of flying but was sent off course by the thought of all the studies needed in science and maths. He eventually went for a career in journalism and gained experience by reading the weekend news on *Isle of Wight Radio*. Then he moved to several mainland BBC stations.

Tom grew up on the Island and was educated at Totland Primary, Bembridge School and Ryde School. In his pursuit of a career in journalism he studied at Westminster University.

Thanks to Captain Stephen Bruh, Tom suddenly took a different flight path and was able to obtain a place on a flying course. Suddenly, that Heathrow dream had become more of a reality. His 18 month integrated course, under the guidance of CTC Aviation Training, included a year in New Zealand learning to fly in small planes.

Tom knew he'd finally achieved the impossible dream when he took an easyJet Airbus into the skies around Gatwick Airport – and there was not a drone in sight.

"I still tingle with excitement and my heart starts beating faster at just the thought of it. It was a brilliantly clear day with no cloud or wind. It was almost too easy in those ideal conditions. All of a sudden I was in charge of all that engine power."

When I decided to record an interview with Tom for both the radio station and *The Beacon*, he came up with an intriguing suggestion. Would I like to interview him in Southampton, where they trained pilots to fly the Airbus? Little did I realise that as soon as my recorder was switched on, I was to be invited to take the controls. Thankfully, it was a land-based simulator.

I was given a quick lesson and then Gatwick Airport loomed up on a giant screen. It was over to me. I was hopeless and on one occasion I came within 200 feet of the ground. This brought on every warning light and the cabin's sirens screeched. Apparently, I didn't pass. The kind instructor took pity on me and gave me a much higher mark than I deserved.

Tom, who is now with Virgin Airways, flies all around the world. Prior to the day we met in Southampton, Tom had already spent 2,500 hours flying an Airbus. On the actual the day before our interview he had flown 3000 miles with return trips to both Rome and Zurich.

He is full of surprises and has written a play and has hopes a famous actor may take the lead in it. During his broadcasting career he made a superb documentary to mark the 30th anniversary of the Moorgate tube disaster. Edited highlights were heard on a 100 British radio stations.

I have a favourite Island story – and it wasn't by Royal Appointment. Our intrepid young *IW Radio* news reporter, a certain Tom Clifton, was sent to the Havenstreet Steam Railway to cover a visit by our Queen. Naively, and to the dismay of seasoned Royal reporters, he asked Her Majesty if she'd enjoyed her train ride.

"Suddenly the security guys jumped on me and grabbed the tape. I think they thought my microphone was something more sinister and I expected to be arrested. They took my name and details and I understand I'm still on a Buckingham Palace black list for breaking journalistic protocol."

In fact, Ma'am gracefully replied that she had enjoyed it and thanked him for asking.

CHAPTER 85

Richard Frame

WHEN DR FRAME was my GP at the Shanklin Medical Centre, on my occasional visits I would get the updates on just what his son Richard was currently doing in the world of showbusiness. A year or two earlier, when he was still a schoolboy, we had all known of the occasion he had danced with Michael Jackson at the 1996 Brit Awards.

When he came on my radio show he told the story of the day he went to the London auditions for the Brit Awards to be in the group to dance with an un-named American international artist. Then came two surprises. He expected about a 100 to be there but it turned out to be 500. When they were told it was going to be with Michael Jackson you could not have topped the excitement.

"Michael was quite friendly and more so than I had expected him to be. I had a couple of conversations with him and during one I asked him why he wore white plasters on his right hand. He revealed that when he danced, his head followed his hands. He was such a great professional.

"On the night I think he was quite nervous because of the London IRA bombings around that time," said Richard.

A few years later, when Richard was firmly established in the entertainment business, I caught up with him again at the Chichester Festival Theatre. There he was in his element playing in *Blue Remembered Hills*. His character of Raymond was just seven years old. In this classic play all the adults play children. He wore short trousers, a cowboy hat, holster, gun and sheriff's badge.

"Raymond struggles to talk the whole time and I just lose myself in the character. I've had to study perfecting a stammer and I went right to the top and watched Colin Firth in *The King's Speech*."

Richard has also had some quality television experience. He'd been seen in *Wire On The Blood*, *The Bill*, *Hope And Glory*, *Family Affairs*, *Kingdom*, *The Hollow Crown*, which starred another Islander in Jeremy Irons, and *Holby*.

He also appeared in several huge West End shows including the award-winning *Our House*. In between his television appearances he's toured Britain in several productions for the Propeller Theatre Company.

Richard, who attended Ryde School, is always so grateful for the opportunities given to him at Shanklin Theatre by David Redston and Tony Wright. It was shows like *Mame* and *Notre Dame* that inspired him to aim for an acting career.

"Growing up on the Island gives you more of an identity. When you are in London there are so many people and you can lose the confidence the Island gives its potential young stars."

In more recent times Richard joined London's West End production of *The Lion King*, playing Timon, and stayed there for several years. In 2017 he found time to make a brief appearance in *EastEnders*.

When he was a member of Shanklin Theatre's Stagecoach Theatre School he had two major dreams. One was to appear in a West End show and the other was to appear on television. Dreams can come true, as several of his old contemporaries at Shanklin Theatre have also found out.

So, the career of Richard Frame has just been what the doctor ordered. During his career Richard has had great support from his parents.

CHAPTER 86

Steve Porter

WHEN WE HAD FAMILY HOLIDAYS back in the 80s one of our games on long journeys was to spot Eddie Stobart lorries. Meanwhile, back on the Island a guy called Steve Porter had just about purchased a glorified pick-up truck – and his overdraft was just £500. He'd been a driver for the Temperature factory at Lake and his local friends in haulage thought he was insane leaving a well paid job to go out on his own. Now, with just two of us in the car, I love spotting Steve Porter lorries across southern England and occasionally beyond. A year or two ago, from a train window, I noticed a huge Steve Porter depot at Hilsea. I felt quite proud.

During my whole life I have been inspired by ordinary local people who have bravely ventured forth and achieved well deserved success. Steve Porter is the perfect example. Like a true Islander, it's not gone to his head, either.

It was back in 1981 when he bought his old green van and headed for the Island's country lanes. That was the birth of Steve Porter Transport. Now he's got a staff of around 50, at least a dozen trucks and over 25 trailers. His name is known by thousands of Islanders. Let's head back to '81. It was the year Prince Charles and Lady Diana Spencer were married and John Lennon topped the pop charts with *Imagine*.

"I'd got to the age of 25 and used to go out for nights with other drivers. One evening I saw one driver and I thought he looks 65 but must be only 45. I wasn't sure I wanted to be stuck in that job for my whole life. So I decided to start my own business and control my own destiny. That's how it all started.

"My ambition was to have my own truck, get another for my middle brother Andy and let my youngest brother Tim run the office," revealed Steve. Those hopes were all realised.

The glory days of haulage had been a few decades earlier and life was tough but he stuck at it and suddenly his business began to thrive – and his overdraft limit was a little more than £500.

There were a few stories to relate. The company had to deliver some live snakes to London. The driver kept their container in his cab. When he went to deliver them he noticed a small nine inch snake on the floor – and then he spotted a few more. In desperation, they had to get someone from the Island brave enough to look for them. He found 14 in the end.

Steve grew up in Gurnard and I asked him for any memories of his childhood – long before the days of health and safety.

"I can remember when I was about eight, three of us built a boat called *Matchbox*. Well actually, it was an upturned wardrobe with a broomstick for a mast and a sheet for a sail. The three of us used to go halfway across Gurnard Bay in that. We must have been crazy. No wonder my father lost his hair by the age of 30."

In more recent times Steve served as the president of the IW Chamber of Commerce and would attend as many meetings as he could.

"The office staff never seemed to mind me going to meetings. I think they were glad to get rid of me. Luckily, I have always been surrounded by people who do their jobs better than me."

Away from the company, Steve loves fishing in his boat, although his wife often has more success than him, and old motorbikes. When he was 50 he undertook his first circuit race on a motorbike. He has also raced cars.

CHAPTER 87

Maurice Gilliam

FOR SEVERAL YEARS I met up with Maurice Gilliam on a regular basis. These were not prearranged meetings but, in most cases, we were at the same local amateur stage productions. We saw both good – and not so good. I was luckier than Maurice. I was covering for the IW Amateur Theatre Awards and only had to see a show once. He was filming the productions and would have to go on several nights and then, I guess, would put the best bits together and make one DVD. On some occasions, I certainly didn't envy him. There were, however, a few that I would loved to have seen more than once. That was not really possible, as sometimes there were four shows in the same week.

Maurice loves his work and is so enthusiastic and conscientious. My late father, Roy, would have been so thrilled to have known that Maurice had put some of his rare old Island home movies on to commercial videos. I still meet up with people who comment on dad's old movies about Island railways.

In 2014 Maurice retired from 40 years on the Island's ambulance service. He's that kind of person who had the qualities to have coped with a job that many of us would find impossible to handle. Well done Maurice for caring so much.

He's come a long way from being a Saturday boy at Henley's Bakery in Seaview. This led to a full time job. When he moved to Reflex in Ryde, who developed photographs, he could never have dreamed that photography would become such a passion later in his life.

After a spell at Ryde's Vectis Laundry he moved to Trucast and his life changed for ever. They were looking for volunteers to train for first aid and that eventually led to his long career in the ambulance service.

"I trained with the Ryde St Johns Ambulance Service and, amongst others, met ambulance drivers and firemen. Later an ambulance came to Trucast and the driver, who I knew from my first aid course, tempted me into trying to join the service.

"It was then run by the Fire Service but I never got a reply. It was eventually taken over by the NHS. In 1974 I replied to an advert in the *County Press* and got the job."

Maurice had never even been inside an ambulance. That changed very quickly and he trained with some very experienced staff. Obviously, crews can be affected by some of their more tragic call outs. They remain so professional. As a family man, he admitted there were times when he just had to let his emotions go. There were happy memories like helping with the birth of a baby, until the midwife arrived.

It's a known fact that there are times when black humour can help ease the stresses of such a difficult job. Maurice explained this to me in our 2015 interview.

"Black humour is almost like a survival thing and helps you hide behind the reality of it all."

For several years Maurice had the well known Island footballer Alan Reed as his crew mate. They enjoyed working together and were an unlikely combination. Alan loved sport and Maurice didn't.

The day Alan died in a tragic accident near Binfield, they'd been in Newport at lunchtime and were due on the evening shift. It was one of the saddest moments of Maurice's life.

In happier moments, Maurice met his lovely wife, Rose, at a 69 Club dance at the Oasis, on Ryde seafront. He's also filmed over 200 Island weddings and around 150 Island amateur shows – which is where we came in.

CHAPTER 88

Roger North

THE FIRST TIME I ever interviewed Roger North he talked non-stop for two hours. Unfortunately, I only had to write 800 words for my Sports Personality column in the *Weekly Post*. Exactly ten years later, following some of his amazing local football successes, I went back for a follow-up. I had more space but still not enough. On *John Hannam Meets* at least we had the ad breaks and news bulletins to stop him. Later, when Northy worked for Pompey's youth set-up, if you met him on the ferry going back to the Island the journey went so quickly.

To be honest, I loved chatting to Roger. He talked a lot of sense and had the success to back it up. I felt sorry for him when he kept taking talented Island youngsters to Fratton Park and few of them made it with the club. Several moved to other clubs and found success in the Football League. He certainly could spot talent.

His initial arrival on the Island was rather low key and he had higher qualifications than anyone else in local football. He told me, back in '78: "When I came here despite my qualifications I almost had to plead to join the Ventnor club. I didn't do any coaching and just played in their reserve team."

When he moved to Shanklin to manage the club, they didn't know what had hit them. Under Roger's guidance they became a team to be feared.

"It was all down to the players and I pushed them hard in training. They may not have looked a good side on paper but they worked so hard and had a go.

"There was only one boss. Players don't pick my teams. I call a spade a spade and my Shanklin lads walked tall and were proud to walk through the town."

Bigger clubs were taking note and he was tempted to Newport to run their reserve team. There he helped to develop quality local players like Andy Rayner, Mark Deacon, Shaun Flux, John Hazell, John Simpkins and his own son Sean. Within a year or two they were starring in the Wessex League for Newport and East Cowes Vics. In that Newport reserve team he had just the kind of experienced old campaigners to bring out the best in the youngsters. Tommy Owen, Bob McColm, Trevor Thorne and John Jupe were among them.

Eventually he moved to East Cowes Vics to team up with Graham Daish and they got to the final of the Hampshire Senior Cup and won the Hampshire League second division. When Graham Daish left the club for a while Roger took over as manager.

Newport tempted him back as first team coach. In 1988 he told me: "They had the best facilities in Hampshire football. You can't create a Church Litten and you just felt the buzz as you walked in the ground." Sadly, St George's Park has never had that same special feel.

Roger went on to take Ryde Sports in a completely different direction and I loved a rather special quote he gave me.

"In the old days they used to hang a sign on the entrance to Portsmouth Harbour. Welcome home – and would you like to sign for Ryde Sports." The Partlands club had always had a reputation for primarily playing mainland players. Roger changed that and played an all-Wight team. They did him proud.

He revealed to me one of his biggest disappointments in local football.

"I was acting manager of Newport and had to pay out £120 in wages to players who had not earned it. They played just to pick up their money after the game."

To someone as honest as the late Roger North that was hard to take. We miss you Northy – and your constant chatter.

CHAPTER 89

Rod Gammons

I KNEW ROD GAMMONS' father long before I met him. His late father, Reg, was a no nonsense impresario and entertainments manager. During his career he pulled down the curtains on big band legend Jack Payne and much later the Pretty Things. Locally, he ran the Ventnor Winter Gardens, the Commodore Theatre, Ryde, and later the Esplanade Pavilion. Rod played in local groups, like Rolled Gold, the Romany Band and the highly acclaimed White Fire Band. He also was a well known Island peripatetic percussion teacher in local schools. Many of his ex-pupils had a shock when he turned up on *Top Of The Pops* playing drums.

Rod bought a bungalow in Brighstone and became a kind of a local Joe Meek. In other words, he turned his Wilberforce Road home into a recording studio. I can remember going there to interview him about some of the local artists he'd recorded. Initially, he had started in Nodehill, Newport, with a Portastudio mini-deck.

At Brighstone he recorded local artists like Ken Phillips on his Dakota Records label and had visiting artists from the mainland. These included Sadie Nine and former Miss United Kingdom runner-up, Lynda Myers. Meanwhile, Rod was still gigging locally as a one-man band at local dinner dances and pubs. His recording skills allowed him to sing, play drums, bass, piano, acoustic guitar and synthesisers, all at the same time. He was particularly popular at the White Mouse, Chale.

In 1984 Rod recorded and produced a legendary Island vinyl album called *Feet On The Street*. It showcased so many brilliant local bands. Among them were the Mechanix, Mumbo Jumbo, Quiet Life, Enforce and the Garage Band.

Ironically, none of them achieved the fame they had been searching for. In fact, it was Rod who became well known for his involvement with several hit records. In '87 he was clearly seen playing drums on *Top Of The Pops* for Hoddle and Waddle. He had recorded and mixed their Top Ten single.

Rod's biggest test came in 1980 when he managed to produce three tracks from a guy with no singing talent at all. It was done for a newspaper story to prove non singers can make records. He surrounded the 'singer' with talented Island musicians like Tim Marshall, Andy Skelton, Tim Muncaster and himself. *Radio Solent* were so impressed and Richard Cartridge played two tracks and interviewed the singer live on air. Did I mention his name? It was John Hannam. No wonder the lead track was *Poor Little Fool*.

After moving to London, Rod's studio was always in demand and he enjoyed another unlikely hit with his pairing of Eartha Kitt and Bronski Beat. Once again it was seen on *Top Of The Pops* and his demand as a pop record producer took another leap forward. In the 90s I was invited up to his studio in Soho which proved a fascinating experience.

Rod was not keen to leave the Island but had to follow the work. Now it's so easy with many home studios and computers to work with.

In more recent years Rod has set up a very successful family business called Rotolight and they have won several awards for their innovative technology. They are based at Pinewood Studios. I was driving there a few years ago and at the very last minute they had to postpone my visit. I hope to get another invite. Rod is the chairman, co-founder and technical director. I wonder if he ever thinks of that Brighstone studio? I still have several records that were made there.

CHAPTER 90

Lauri Say

LAURI SAY CAUSED quite a sensation in 1968 when he brought out an EP vinyl record featuring four tracks about the Island and its people. The satire songs were *The Isle of Wight For Me*, *The Southern Vectis Song*, *The Hovercraft* and UDI *For The Isle of Wight*. Only 99 were released, to save paying purchase tax – or so they thought. In the end the price had to go up from 10/- to 12/11, as they sold up to 5000 copies. In more recent years it's been re-released on CD.

I loved the record and when I began with IW R*adio* in 1990, it was often played on my programmes and a few others. When it first came out I was not a freelance journalist and it was not until 2004 that I managed to finally track down Lauri Say, who had spent nine years on the Island. I caught up with him in Emsworth, just a few miles from Portsmouth.

Lauri, who came here to teach at the IW College, had only sung in the bath before he came here. In the early 60s he went to the original Newport Folk Club, at the Castle Inn, and liked what he saw and heard. He went out and bought a guitar, learnt three chords and began singing there and later at the Redan pub in Ryde. Then came that legendary EP.

"We actually recorded the songs in one evening at a private house in Watergate Road, Newport. Also on the tracks are John Underwood, Roy Middlebrook and John Newman. It was billed as Lauri Say and the Island Folk. Alan Witcombe produced it and John Waterman was the recording supervisor," said Lauri.

It was rumoured that the former Island MP, Mark Woodnutt, who was mentioned on a couple of the tracks, always carried the record with him, particularly if he was talking to the media. Lauri even suggested he believed Mark might not have realised the UDI *For The Isle of Wight* song was a joke. One of the lines said "and we'll have Mark Woodnutt as king." It's a nice story, anyway.

Lauri also revealed to me that he actually wrote the Hovercraft song on a Red Funnel ferry to Southampton. He also told me he was thrilled to become quite famous on the Island. So much so, he was asked by a waitress in the Ryde Wimpy if he was the guy who had released the record. She became even more excited when he signed his autograph "with love from Lauri Say." He was then in his mid-30s and in danger of being an old man to young people. We all know that feeling.

His other memories of the Island included being a Labour councillor on the Newport Borough Council, when his party had the most seats, learning to drive here and being involved with the Foulk brothers at our two huge pop festivals.

As a youngster Lauri was inspired by singer/songwriter Tom Lehrer, who was famous for sick humour songs. Lauri liked his gift of rhyming. In fact, the idea for his local Island songs came from a visit to Wiltshire. He was among 3000 people watching a show by Adge Cutler and the Wurzels. They wrote songs about local people and places and this brought a great response from the audience. Just like Lauri Say and the Island Folk did a year or two later. There were daring lyrics about Bembridge and Seaview, Island buses, getting a girl in the club and the noise of the hovercraft. It would probably be banned now by those goody goody people.

CHAPTER 91

Ray (Olly) Hamilton

THEY USED TO SAY BEWARE of Olly Hamilton, especially if he smiled at you or offered you his business card. Well they would, wouldn't they? He was an undertaker. In fact, Olly was one of those people who, away from his business, could make you smile in an instant. It was a pleasure to meet him in the street, watching his beloved Medina cricket team or working hard at Newport Football Club, entertaining home officials and visiting guests.

The year of 1977 was rather special for him. He won the Newport crib singles championship. Mind you, a few months earlier he'd run around Church Litten football ground clutching the FA Cup. No Newport hadn't achieved the greatest ever soccer miracle – but the Saints had beaten Manchester United to win it in May 1976. Lawrie McMenemy brought his team over to play 'the Port' in a special celebration match.

There was one thing that was kept from the gentlemanly Mr McMenemy.

Olly told me: "The Newport lads were playing with the cup in the bath. Dave Attrill filled it with water and showered himself."

Undertakers are unique people and certainly need to leave their work behind to make life bearable. Olly loved his sport and ballroom dancing. He was the president of Medina Cricket Club for many years and on Saturday nights he would come down to Seaclose Park to see the latter stages of our matches. You knew when he'd arrived as there was always the smell of Brut in the air, as he was on his way to a dance.

I can vividly remember when top scriptwriter Alan Simpson, of Galton and Simpson fame, came for a personal appearance at Ashey's Ponda Rosa roadhouse. I was writing for the *Weekly Post* and interviewed the guy who helped create real comedy television shows like *Hancock* and *Steptoe*. My photographer was looking for a photo opportunity and we didn't have to go very far – Olly Hamilton was on hand. He quickly joined in the fun to be photographed with Alan.

Olly loved fun at social events. I can remember making a speech at a Medina Cricket Club dinner to thank him for all his support of the club, in so many different ways. I told the diners, jokingly, I could now reveal a secret. Olly had won the *Hearse Of The Year Show* at Wembley – and he loved it. In fact, he never missed a club dinner for 12 years. All the gifts for the ladies came out of his own pocket.

When Newport were at their old Church Litten ground, Olly, with help from Dick Hayter, Fred Young and Bill Buckell, had the idea to instigate a clubhouse. It was how or where?

"We turned three old offices under the stand into a club, took turns at the bar but had no till, so we put the money in an old box. It was not the ideal shape, either. Tall drinkers had to stand on the right and shorter ones on the left. We found some old planks for seats," reflected Olly.

Eventually they built on another piece. That start enabled the club to develop a brand new clubhouse with 1000 members and they served lunches.

I love the story of the night Newport won the Hampshire Senior Cup at Fratton Park. He was given the task of getting their rather inebriated goalkeeper Bernie Cullen back home. It was probably just before sunrise! "I stood Bernie up and he fell in the door. I left before his wife came down."

CHAPTER 92

Tony Scott

I'LL NEVER FORGET the first time I met comedian Tony Scott. It was 1979 and the setting was a somewhat run down caravan at Colwell's Fort Warden Holiday Centre. It was surrounded by rabbits and his welcoming cup of coffee took 30 minutes to arrive. He'd forgotten to put the gas on. I had to wait until his cabaret spot had finished and eventually arrived back home long after midnight. Could he talk!! We did become great mates and he lived here for many years.

At that time there was a popular chart hit called *Video Killed The Radio Star*. It certainly didn't apply to Tony Scott. He was a veteran of over 500 broadcasts and had appeared in some huge hit radio series. With no television, they were listened to by millions of people. He appeared on *Variety Bandbox*, *Henry Hall's Guest Night*, *The Vic Oliver Show* and

Variety Playhouse, among many others. In fact he was still working on the strength of them.

Tony was a great tease and often told people he was the brother of Terry Scott, which was way off course. In fact, his father, Bill Scott-Gordon, produced the Sandown Pavilion summer season shows for nine consecutive years. Tony spent his summer holidays here.

He once told me: "My old man gave me one Sunday concert at Sandown Pavilion and Shanklin Theatre. That was the only time I made any money out of him."

Tony was full of stories. He knew Tony Hancock and Benny Hill before they were star names and he starred in a show that included an unknown Max Bygraves, who was earning £14 a week. Scotty was earning a lot more. He did undertake star roles at the Palladium and the Prince of Wales Theatre. They loved him in the States. The gangster fraternity who frequented the nightclubs where he appeared called him 'English'.

I loved his sense of fun. He rang me up one day and told me: "I just had a cheque for four pence from the BBC. They are very honest. One of my old shows was heard in Outer Mongolia."

He frowned on the blue comics and had recently seen a lot of old people walk out on a young comedian, who'd only been in the business for 18 months. "I've known comics who've been out of work longer than that," quipped Tony.

In the 80s Tony went straight – and became a serious actor. He was in the snooker movie *Number One* and appeared in summer seasons at Shanklin Theatre. In 1985 he phoned me up and asked if I would like to interview Mandy Rice-Davies. Silly question, really. Back in the Profumo days that would have been every mans dream. He was touring with her in *A Bedfull Of Foreigners*. In the time between shows at the Kings Theatre, Southsea, Tony and the cast left us two in a dressing room and went for a snack in the cafe next door. No, I won't tell you what happened!

That same year Tony got me an interview I had virtually given up on, after numerous refusals. It was Danny La Rue, who was a personal friend of his. After Dan's Sandown Pavilion show Tony told me to go home but do not go to bed. He went for a post-gig meal with Dan at the Fighting Cocks. The call came at 1.30am and we met at the Cliff Tops Hotel a few hours later. Ironically, Danny and I became friends up until he died. That was all due to Tony Scott.

CHAPTER 93

Sam Twining

IN AUGUST 2000 Heather and I received an unexpected late invitation to a special Cowes Week dinner in Northwood House. It was definitely a posh suit night and my array of brightly coloured jeans stayed in the wardrobe. We wondered just whose table we would be sat on. We found ourselves in the delightful company of Sam and Anne Twining. It was during his reign as the Island's High Sherriff. I was flattered that he even knew who I was – so I waited for at least ten minutes before I invited him on to my radio show. He accepted straight away.

Due to his many commitments it took some time and it was in January 2001 when he came live on to my show. Ironically, between the Northwood House dinner and our show date, we had again met Sam at a couple of functions in his beloved St Lawrence. One was the opening of the revamped village hall and the other at a village flower show. The *John Hannam Meets* was a Tea Special. In the first hour I had three famous singing brothers, Peter Sarstedt, Robin Sarstedt and Eden Kane, whose parents had worked on a tea plantation in India. Sam was my second hour guest.

On the Sunday lunchtime the radio station was very quiet – and, embarrassingly, we had no tea in the kitchen. At least I'd had my Twinings Earl Grey with my breakfast and Sam had already enjoyed his cups of Twinings English Breakfast tea.

Sam, a perfect English gentleman, apparently was used to drinking up to 15 cups of tea a day. These included several different blends to suit his palate and the time of day.

Originally, Sam thought about nothing else other than a career in the Royal Marines. His dream had come true and he spent 17 happy years of his life in that world famous unit. That life led him to join the family business.

"When I was serving in East Africa I was privileged to have the opportunity to travel around and I saw a lot of tea and coffee growing. I was fascinated by the horticultural side of the business. That really helped me to understand it and I spent all the leave I had earned going to India and Sri Lanka (then Ceylon) to see how tea was grown."

When his joined Twinings in 1956 and was learning how to taste tea, he had the enormous advantage of knowing what the plant looked like and how they turned it into tea. Only two of the staff had ever been to a tea plantation and one of those was his father. He quickly moved from being a pot boy to a tea taster.

Sam is such a tea historian and he had so many facts in his head and could instantly relate them. Over the years he'd been all around the world talking about tea.

The correct way is to put the milk in first and he hinted that putting a tea earn on the pot can keep it too hot and give the effect of stewed tea.

What did he do when confronted with stewed tea? "I just raise my eyebrows and say nothing."

I was also fascinated to know that Queen Victoria was the person who made afternoon tea so popular. One of her staff had come up with the original idea.

At the time of our interview Twinings had 150 blends of different tea, 12 herbal varieties and ten fruit teas.

Sam loved the experience of being our High Sherriff.

"Both Anne and myself are Islanders but we both went to places we've never been before. We met lots of people doing great things for the Island."

He went home to a cup of Twinings Darjeeling and I settled for Lady Grey and a cherry bakewell in the Round House Tea Room.

CHAPTER 94

Michelle Magorian

WHEN I FIRST MET a very charming lady called Michelle Magorian at her Bembridge home it was to plan her appearance on my radio show. I left feeling rather sorry for her. She was clearly struggling to bring up her two boys, after the break-up of her marriage. We became friends and I just hoped her life would take an upturn, as I felt she would certainly deserve it.

The night of October 25, 1998, changed her life for ever. It was the evening her novel, *Goodnight Mr Tom*, was seen on television in a dramatisation starring John Thaw. I could barely wait for the end credits before ringing her with my congratulations. I was one of millions who had been captivated by the brilliant production. It certainly had been a tearjerker. In fact, it was watched by the biggest television audience of the year.

That was just the start. It was quickly repeated, by public demand, there was a number one DVD, it won seven television awards and both a play and a musical followed. There was also an audio book and it has been serialised on national radio.

"I actually started to write *Goodnight Mr Tom* at a novel writing class and in the end it took me five years to complete. Some of the ideas were based on wartime stories my mother had told me."

The only disappointment was that due to the impact the show had made on her life, she had to leave the Island to be nearer the action. She was flooded with work but it was all on the mainland. Being a single parent with two young boys and no maintenance coming in, meant there was no way she could commute.

A few years later I met her at the Chichester Festival Theatre and she was still rueing the fact she had to leave the Island.

"I miss all the wonderful views on the Island but most of all the people. Many of them I met by sheer chance but they were so marvellous. There is something about the Island that brings the best out of people. It was certainly the best place to get a divorce. The people really brought me round."

Back to that first viewing of *Goodnight Mr Tom*. The success of the television drama saw the novel republished and in some places around Britain it became the best selling children's book over the Christmas period.

The stage version won an Olivier Award for the Best Entertainment and Family Production, following its triumphant run at London's Phoenix Theatre

Another of Michelle's books, *Back Home*, has been seen in two separate television adaptations. One starred Hayley Mills, which was a hit in America, and the other featured Sarah Lancashire. Whilst on the Island one of her other novels, *Just Henry*, was seen on a New Year's Eve transmission. This one starred Island-born Sheila Hancock, whose late husband John Thaw was so magnificent in *Goodnight Mr Tom*, Josh Bolt and Barbara Flynn. During our last interview Michelle revealed she has had eight novels published plus two poetry books and two collections of short stories.

Before Michelle left the Island she made a return to the stage with local appearances. Since then she's been in demand for mainland lectures and appearances.

She is also a gifted lyric writer and singer Joanna Forbes L'Estrange has recorded some of her songs. Several of which were actually written on the Island.

I still watch *Goodnight Mr Tom* on a regular basis – and always shed a few tears in the same places. There is a double happy ending, too. In the TV drama and Michelle's life.

CHAPTER 95

Vic Lewis

WHEN HE WAS 40 Vic Lewis gave up playing cricket for Newport first XI to make way for a younger man. He had no plans to make any sort of comeback – or so he thought. Five years later a few friends from the Newport Victoria Tennis Club persuaded him to come out of retirement to play for their evening cricket team. He didn't take much persuading and was still playing 30 years later, after taking 300 wickets or more.

That success with Victoria led to weekend league cricket with Godshill. He formed an ageless bowling quartet whose combined ages were over 200 years. Just for the record they were John Batten, Ronnie Denness, Vic and John Hannam. Rumours suggest John H was the youngest!

Vic, who sadly died in 2018, was such fun in the dressing room, with his ready wit and boyish enthusiasm. He sometimes defied his age with rash challenges to team mates. On one occasion, on a big match day, he took the bait from Pete Urry for a race across the pitch.

"It was neck and neck and I'm sure Peter stuck his foot out and sent me tumbling. I ended up in hospital anyway," revealed Vic, when I interviewed him for my *County Press* Sportrait column in 2002.

A year or two later he was bowling for Victoria on the Seaclose matted concrete wicket and suddenly went sprawling. He crumbled into a heap and all but one of his team mates crowded round him. The one who kept his distance just happened to be a surgeon from St Mary's Hospital, who was clearly off duty and did not want to know. The intrepid Lewis soon recovered.

Vic was a gifted sportsman. Carisbrooke-born, he reached the finals of the ABA youth boxing championships at Wembley. At 16, he was six foot tall and 9 stone 9lb. After national service he worked at Saunders-Roe and played cricket for East Cowes. He was a handful on their notorious bituturf wicket. In one memorable game he took 8 for 9. Once, while fielding in the slips, he was hit on the head by the ball and was out cold for a minute or so. He came round to find a new batsmen at the crease. The ball had been safely caught direct from Vic's head.

Vic with his wife Pat

He played in a superb Newport team who were in a class of their own. Despite trying to convince everyone he could bat a bit, he seldom got the chance with Keith Mitchell and co at the top of their batting order. He was one of their canny array of fast bowlers.

Late in his career he played for Porchfield – and was in the wars again. He was hit by the ball and ended up with a broken palate bone in his face and a smashed cheek bone, which even moved a little.

"Our skipper, Ray Hayward, came to see me in hospital that night and reminded me I hadn't paid my tea money!"

Pat, his lovely wife, always gave him great support and he appreciated that so much. Every Friday morning in Sainsbury's she also let him off the shopping. While she was filling the trolley he was perusing the daily papers and magazines. I tried it, too. I was not so lucky!

We gave Vic a great send off with a celebration of his life at the Newclose cricket ground. We had some wonderful memories to savour.

I can remember the day at the Godshill ground when Vic was fielding in the deep and a batsmen hit the ball into his area. He must have visually lost the ball, as he ran completely in the other direction – much to the amusement of both teams.

CHAPTER 96

Ron Sheppard

LINDA COUCH, a former boss of IW *Radio*, called me into her office and suggested that a well known local fundraiser, by the name of Ron Sheppard, would be an interesting guest on my radio show. Apparently, he also had a showbiz background. At that time he was the chairman of the Island's Arachnoiditis Self-Help Group. He was also one of our earliest fundraisers for the MRI Scanner. Little did I realise that in future years he would come back on my show as Britain's most married man.

In fact, I've had a hard job to keep track of his marriages. I think, as I write this chapter in January 2019, it has been eight times. It could be nine by the time you read this. I went to one of them.

Once you become a friend of Ron Sheppard it's hard to dodge him – but I've never wanted to. I have so many memories of interviews with him. When he lived on the Island, Ron loved to discover and help burgeoning young local talent. I can remember him doing so much to publicise a young singer called Samantha Wakeman. He brought her on my show to be interviewed.

I had seen Ron perform long before I met him. He was a Pontins' Bluecoat from 1981 and had a season or two at their Little Canada Centre at Wootton. The campers loved him and he had no trouble in dating young ladies, with so many on site. During one season an unknown young Bluecoat called Shane Richie worked at the centre. Ron has always told me they got up to mischief. Shane has never confirmed this but he has cracked a few gags about Ron's regular trips to the altar.

A young Ron Sheppard first came to the Island in 1962. They stayed at the Atherfield Bay Holiday Camp and he was so impressed with their entertainments staff. That was the reason, a few years later, he eventually went to Pontins. One of the Military Road team turned out to be a kind of mentor for Ron. This guy was working his first-ever professional engagement. He had been a draughtsman. It was Roy Barraclough.

Ron came back here four years later to initially work for Warners at their St Clare Centre at Puckpool. He met his first wife, Margaret, at that centre.

In 1993 he moved permanently to the Island with his fifth wife, Sue. I got to know her as a very popular carer at the Osborne Cottage Residential home in East Cowes, where my lovely mum spent the last years of her life. It was some time before she told me who she was married to.

Ron was often used as a kind of bait by Alex Dyke, during his days on IW *Radio*. He must have enjoyed it because he often went back for more.

After he left the Island, Bertie and I were invited to his Somerset home. At that time he was very happy with his eighth wife, Weng. We had a great time and they were the perfect hosts. I must admit I was so sad when they parted. Weng was so good for him.

Since then, Ron's controversial book, *The Lord Of The Wedding Rings*, has been published. He's also been featured in huge spreads in national papers and has made several television appearances. There is now talk of his life story being made into a movie. The last thing I heard was that it was going to be called *The Wife Collector*.

Ron has had his fair share of critics in past years. I have experienced a different side to him. When Heather died in 2006, he phoned me more than anyone to see how I was coping. I have never forgotten that. Thanks Ron.

CHAPTER 97

Richard Stone

I KNEW THE NAME of Richard Stone as a show producer and theatrical agent but had never met him. Some famous stars I'd interviewed mentioned how important he'd been in their careers and a few even told me he lived at Seaview. There was only one person who could confirm this – as he knew everyone who lived in the village. Yes, Nobby Nash did come up trumps. He and his wife Liz even kept an eye on the house when Richard and Sara were away.

This led me to the man whose client list had included Benny Hill, Terry Scott, Victoria Wood and Dave Allen. I was so excited to meet him and interview him for my radio show. We hit if off straight away and kept in touch. At the time he was trying to finish his book, *You Should Have Been In Last Night*.

Sadly, Richard was diagnosed with cancer and I think the desire to complete the book kept him alive. He died shortly after the launch, which was held at the Green Room Club in London. I was flattered to even be invited and there were stars everywhere, including June Whitfield, Andrew Sachs, Dave Allen and David Jason. Richard was keen for me to interview one or two of the famous guests. Dave Allen instantly agreed but Mr Jason wouldn't do it. Sadly, the next time I met the wonderful Dave Allen was just a few weeks later at Richard's funeral in Seaview. We walked together and chatted en route to the wake.

I'll never forget the Saturday morning in August 2000 when Richard rang me and asked if I could be at his Seaview home within an hour. Before I could ask why, he said: "Victoria Wood is at my house with her son Henry and they are going to Robin Hill. She is happy to talk to you if you can get here quickly." Heather didn't want to miss out so any thoughts of lunch were abandoned and we headed to Seaview. Victoria told me that Richard was the only person to have faith in her during her early struggles to make a name in the business.

Richard was in showbusiness before the war and actually met Sara in a summer show in Saltburn in Yorkshire. War broke out two weeks before the end of the season and they had to paint the glass roof black to be allowed to keep going. Within a few months he was in the army and served in Italy and Africa. He was awarded the Military Cross after gallant action in the Middle East.

After being wounded, and with his entertainment background, Capt Stone was chosen to lead the *Stars In Battledress* shows to entertain our troops at the D-Day landings.

"On D-Day plus four I found myself on a tank landing craft leading the most absurd army to ever go into battle, with people like Terry Thomas, Arthur Haynes and Charlie Chester. With enemy shells exploding all around us we waded ashore carrying props, instruments and dragging mini pianos," said Richard, who later was promoted to Colonel.

In one show a young Benny Hill had been told not to do his act, just feed the principal comic. Richard's predecessor had thought Benny was unfunny. Richard was impressed and changed all that and after the war he became an agent and signed Benny up. The world famous comedian stayed with him for his whole career.

Two quick stories. He once took Dave Allen to America's *Ed Sullivan Show*. His act was passed by Sullivan's son-in-law but nearer transmission the boss himself didn't like it. Allen walked out and headed for England, with Richard in tow.

When the makers of *Goldfinger* forgot to put Shirley Eaton's name on the original credits, she was the lady painted gold, he obtained her far more money than she got paid for the movie, for compensation.

CHAPTER 98

Tony Wheatley

IN 2017 I WAS ASKED if I would be interested in interviewing a great musician called Dennis Greaves, from Nine Below Zero, to promote their forthcoming gig at Newport's Medina Theatre. I agreed and was invited to meet him at a private house in Binstead. It was very successful and I came away very excited to be going back a couple of weeks later to interview the guy who actually owned the house. That was Tony Wheatley. His story included Whitney Houston, Elvis Costello, Blondie, Tom Jones and Rod Stewart. He'd helped to sell millions of records.

Tony and I have become friends and his knowledge about the music business is incredible. He is full of surprises, too. In my first book, I'd written a chapter on the original James Bond guitarist Vic Flick, once of the John Barry Seven and revealed I had been searching for Vic's vinyl solo album, *West Of Windward*, for at least 20 years. It was so rare. Tony found me one.

In 1972 Tony was living on the mainland and got a Saturday job in a record shop. For his interview he was given a record by Charley Pride and told to file it. He passed the test with flying colours. Charley was one of the few black country singers and Tony knew that. The boss had two stores and in the other one Ronnie Wood used to go in and practice, after shop hours. He was in a local band called the Birds at that time.

On leaving school Tony had a boring two years in banking. Looking for more of an exciting life he joined a company called Record Merchandisers. They were distributors and initially his job was to set up new record departments in supermarkets and other non-traditional outlets for music. They had the support of all the top record companies. Then he got promoted to become a sales rep with a company car. This fast-growing company could sell about 40% of any artist's records in the UK. In some cases they could make or break a record.

"I loved soul music and was aware of a brilliant new album by a lady called Whitney Houston. I managed to get an import copy from Arista Records. The guy who came in to try and sell it to me, expected a hard sell but I knew all about it. I told him we would convince our customers to stock this record. We got in early and placed a sizeable order and the rest is history. The independents and others like HMV and Our Price didn't support the album. We sold well over half a million copies – and they even presented me with a gold disc."

Tony would sell such a variety of artists, from Motorhead to Don Estelle and even a Miss World. When Mary Stavin, from Sweden, was Miss World she made a record and he took her around for a promotional day, in his Cortina Estate. If he was hoping for a date – it didn't work out. At the end of the day she asked him to take her to her boyfriend's house. It was footballer Don Shanks of QPR.

When Tony was asked to work on a Woolworth Christmas commercial he had the idea to get Rod Stewart. He agreed to do it and Tony was at the Wembley studio where he recorded it. He'd given Rod a script but he didn't stick to it. It worked like a dream and Rod sold thousands of his *Greatest Hits* album.

Tony, who now has his own company, Resolution, has also worked for Demon Records and Chrysalis Records, amongst others.

Having worked with Nine Below Zero, Tony brought them to the Island – and it was a great night.

CHAPTER 99

John Young

JOHN YOUNG WAS ONE of those Islanders who was so enthusiastic in whatever he did. Whether it was on stage for the Palmerston Players, conjuring up magic tricks for a roomful of children, commentating on Shanklin Regatta shore sports or selling you a flashy shirt and tie in his Trueman's gents outfitters. His fame even spread as far as Blackpool. Once, while on holiday there, a lady stopped him in the street and asked: "Aren't you that magician from the Isle of Wight?"

I once described him as a jack of all trades – and he was. His lifetime achievements included being the founder chairman of Shanklin Round Table, a past chairman of the Shanklin Business Association, being a notable local archer and deep sea fisherman.

There is no doubt John was stage-struck when he joined the town's Palmerston Players, back in the 50s. Initially, he was a backstage operator until a guy in the cast, who was playing a policeman, went sick and John had to make his stage debut. He had six words – and rumours suggested three of them were "ello ello ello."

This quickly led to promotion and he played a bishop in *Pools Paradise*. Then came *See How They Run* and *Love's A Luxury*. For the complete first act of one show John had to portray a dead man in a wheelchair, with his back to the audience. Most of the time he was making faces at the cast to make them laugh. Sometimes they had dress rehearsals at one of our prisons. He loved all that, particularly when they jeered the detective and wolf whistled the ladies.

Many years before his own stage debut, John, in his schoolboy short trousers, would stand in the wings at Sandown Pavilion and marvel at the illusions of George Grimmond in Bill Scott-Gordon's Revels company. In 1947 he was given his first magic set and in the mid-70s he bought one for his own daughter. Well that was his excuse, anyway. With Sy and Isa Lyn's magic shop almost next door to Trueman's, it was no surprise when John became a serious magician. He was also the secretary of the newly formed Vectis Magicians Club. That led John to local holiday centres as an entertainer. In the summer of '81 he worked up to 25 small hotels and played to 150 kids at Ladbroke's Fort Warden.

When he was the chairman of the Shanklin Business Association he came up with the idea of a local pantomime at Shanklin Theatre. It was no real surprise when he regularly played the dame. It was always fun but seemed to go on for hours. In the end punters took sandwiches!

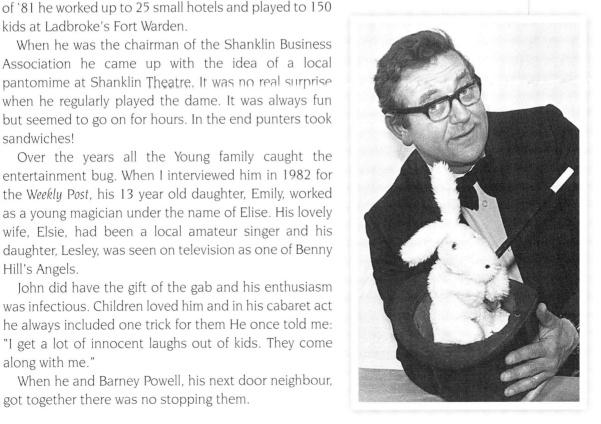

Over the years all the Young family caught the entertainment bug. When I interviewed him in 1982 for the *Weekly Post*, his 13 year old daughter, Emily, worked as a young magician under the name of Elise. His lovely wife, Elsie, had been a local amateur singer and his daughter, Lesley, was seen on television as one of Benny Hill's Angels.

John did have the gift of the gab and his enthusiasm was infectious. Children loved him and in his cabaret act he always included one trick for them He once told me: "I get a lot of innocent laughs out of kids. They come along with me."

When he and Barney Powell, his next door neighbour, got together there was no stopping them.

CHAPTER 100

Mary Ralph

OVER THE YEARS I have enjoyed reading the poems of our own Mary Ralph. I've never wanted to tag her as the Island's answer to Pam Ayres. I am an admirer of both of them. I once spent a brilliant afternoon at Pam Ayres home in Gloucestershire and she was on my original wish list for an interview. I've also enjoyed interviewing Mary on several occasions. I love the story behind her Gladys' Hoover poem.

"I was hoovering the dog one day because when he was a puppy he was terrified of the hoover. To try and stop this I used to rub the brush nozzle of the cleaner all over him and he got to love this. Then he got excited every time I got it out of the cupboard. Then I thought if someone was looking through my window they might think I was rather strange or house proud.

"This inspired me to write a poem about a house proud lady who hoovered everything in sight."

Suddenly Mary began to appear at various venues around the Island reading her poems and many of these were charity shows. This success led her to publish a series of books which became very popular. She even coaxed the late Island-based movie and television actor Michael Sheard into writing a foreword to one of them.

Her audiences quickly decided their own personal favourites. These included A Teenage Daughter, which was close to home, The Dream Of Billy Ray, about former IW *Radio* presenter Bill Padley, and Grandad's Garden, based on a story her father had told her.

On the tenth anniversary of my radio show Mary came in live with a brand new poem.

Oh! The stars and celebrities
John Hannam has met,
Have filled a book
That's hard to forget.
For John has a passion
Toward show business pro's
And a warmth that is genuine
For local heroes

On Isle of Wight Radio,
On John Hannam Meets,
Listeners are thrilled
By each guest that he greets.
A welcome for all
Is John's guarantee,
Whether it's Sir Cliff,
Prince Edward, Or little old me.

Yes, I've sat in his studio
With knees all a-knock,
Hoping me poems
Don't give listeners a shock,
For John Hannam Meets
Is a show of renown,
And I'd be the last one
To let dear old John down.

His programme has run
For ten wonderful years,
Ten years of laughter,
Entertainment and tears
And another ten years
Is my definite choice,
For I can't get enough
Of his sensuous voice.

So it remains to say, Thank you,
To John for each guest,
Ken Dodd with his tickling stick
And Sam Fox with her ..... chest,
Mark King and Craig Douglas,
Local lads who found fame,
And other celebrities
Too many to name.

But whatever their station,
And whoever they are,
John always makes sure
Every guest is a star.

Mary Ralf, 2000.

Luckily, people can't see you blushing when you're on-air.

Mary worked at Sandown High School and every time she wrote a poem she took it in to read to Eileen Toms, one of her colleagues. If she laughed in the right places Mary knew it would work.

One of Mary's greatest moments was when she read a special Valentine's Day love poem, dedicated to her husband John, on BBC1 television.

Mary was keen to praise the late Doug Hayles (stage name Arthur Douglas) who had encouraged her so much and put her in many of his local charity shows.

The Hannam Archives

The following pages of photographs are from the
Hannam Archives featuring groups, bands and
entertainers from John's lifetime writing exploits for the
County Press and IW *Weekly Post*.
These are John's own personal tributes to all of them.
They all have made an impression on the
Island's entertainment scene.

9th Street ▶

◀
*The Cherokees at
the* Medway Queen

◀ *Colin Ellis*

Fatal Dose ▶

◀ *Sybil Johns*

▶
Geoffrey Reed

Mumbo Jumbo

The Yorkies

Garage Band

The Stack

The Knights

The Mechanix

Skyline

Cassie

The Five Alive

Beggars Farm

Blue Moon

Bobby I Can Fly

Buster String Band

The Royals

Lips

The Havens Showband

Figurehead

The Invaders

The Waltons

The Pumphouse Gang

Times Creation

Channel 5

Opus Four

Sharpe and Betchley

Dallas

Abandon City

Quadrant

Castle Jazz Band

Cowes Concert Band

Gloria Roberts Dancers

Ryde Pavilion Summer Season Cast

Island Magicians

Peter Dibbens   Pete Cotton

Signal Box 5

Medina City Jazz Band

Jerry Cahill

Fiona Groves

Bob Roberts

Tony Moroni

Guy Reed

Phil Thomas

Yakajax

Over The Hill Mob

Sky Blue Two

Eric Stevens

Vision

Clare Bonsu

Rockin' Dave

Jack Richards

Brian Martin

Graeme Du Fresne

Larrington Walker

Duncan Jones

The Escorts

Rendezvous

And Finally – Happy Memories for John

Cowes Secondary Modern Juniors

Godshill Cricket Club

East Cowes Vics Football Club

Visiting Sports Panel for Albany Prison.